LOI
NICKEL DIE I
COOKBOOK
FOR BEGINNERS

Mastering Systemic Nickel Allergy: A Comprehensive
Guide with Easy, Flavorful Recipes
Perfect for Beginners

BECKY MATHEW-SMITH

DISCLAIMER:

The information in this book should not be used to diagnose or treat any medical condition. Not every diet and exercise regimen is suitable for everyone. Before beginning any diet, taking any medication, or beginning any fitness or weight- training program, you should always consult with a competent medical expert. The author and publisher expressly disclaim all liability that may arise directly or indirectly from the use of this book. When using kitchen tools, operating ovens and burners, and handling raw food, always use common sense and safety precautions. Readers are encouraged to seek professional assistance when necessary. This guide is provided for informational purposes only, and the author accepts no liability for any liabilities coming from the use of this information.

Printed in the United States of America.
First Edition: January 2024

About The Author: Becky Mathew-Smith

Becky Mathew-Smith, the insightful and compassionate author behind "The Low-Nickel Diet Cookbook for Beginners." is a distinguished figure in the realm of nutrition and holistic well-being. Armed with a deep passion for empowering individuals to lead healthier lives, Becky's expertise extends into the intricate balance of nutrition, allergy management, and the art of mindful living.

A certified nutritionist and culinary expert, Becky Mathew-Smith brings a wealth of knowledge to her readers, intertwining her professional insights with a genuine understanding of the human experience. Her journey with Emily, chronicled in the pages of this transformative narrative, showcases not only her technical proficiency but also her commitment to guiding individuals through the challenges of managing health conditions.

With a knack for crafting delectable recipes tailored to specific dietary needs, Becky's culinary prowess shines through in her acclaimed work, "The Low-Nickel Diet Cookbook for Beginners." Beyond the kitchen, she extends her expertise to offer comprehensive insights into the holistic aspects of well-being, proving that vibrant living is not just an aspiration but an achievable reality.

Becky Mathew-Smith's commitment to health, paired with her empathetic approach, cements her status as a trusted guide in the journey toward wellness. Through her words and culinary creations, she continues to inspire individuals to embrace a life of nourishment, resilience, and vibrant living.

TABLE OF CONTENT

INTRODUCTION

In the heart of Boston's bustling streets, there lived Emily – a 32-year-old woman whose vibrant spirit mirrored the rhythm of the city she called home. Life for Emily was an intricate dance of laughter, family, and the comforting hum of everyday existence. Yet, beneath her cheerful exterior, a silent battle waged on, as Emily grappled with a foe she hadn't anticipated – nickel allergy.

The journey began with subtle discomforts that gradually evolved into a perplexing mystery, marked by unexplained skin reactions and persistent discomfort. Emily, determined to uncover the source of her malaise, embarked on a journey through doctor's appointments and medical consultations. The revelation was both a relief and a challenge – nickel allergy, an unexpected adversary that threatened to cast a shadow over Emily's effervescent approach to life.

Undeterred, Emily faced this unforeseen obstacle with resilience and a determination to thrive despite the limitations. The quest for answers led her to a crossroads where medical knowledge intersected with the profound impact of nutrition and lifestyle. Emily's journey of understanding and transformation unfolded against the backdrop of a city that never slept, mirroring the quiet strength that pulsed within her.

Enter Becky Mathew-Smith, a beacon of expertise in nutrition and holistic wellness. In the gentle guidance of Becky, Emily discovered not only a pathway to manage her nickel allergy but a lifeline that would redefine her relationship with food and flavor.

As the story of Emily's challenges and triumphs unfolds in "Low Nickel Diet Cookbook for Beginners: Mastering Systemic Nickel Allergy: A Comprehensive Guide with Easy, Flavorful Recipes Perfect for Beginners," the pages resonate with a deeply human tone. It's a narrative not just of medical victories but of emotional resilience and the fragility of the human spirit. Each recipe within the book becomes a testament to Emily's journey – a journey that transcends the clinical realm and dives deep into the emotional currents of a woman determined to reclaim her joy.

The culinary odyssey described in the book is not just a list of ingredients and instructions; it's a narrative of hope, courage, and the emotional nuances of overcoming a health challenge. Through Emily's eyes, readers are invited to experience the warmth of a morning nourished by wholesome breakfasts and the comfort of dinners rich in flavors that defy the boundaries of dietary restrictions.

In the end, Emily stands not only as a survivor but as a living testament to the transformative power of embracing challenges with humanity, courage, and the simple joy of savoring each flavorful moment. As readers embark on this emotional journey within the pages of " Low Nickel Diet Cookbook For Beginners," they're not just learning about a low-nickel diet; they're stepping into a narrative that celebrates the resilience of the human spirit.

CHAPTER ONE
UNVEILING NICKEL FREEDOM

Becky Mathew-Smith's Culinary Odyssey

Becky Mathew-Smith's Culinary Odyssey is a captivating exploration into the heart of flavor, health, and the transformative power of nutrition. In this culinary narrative, Becky Mathew-Smith, a seasoned expert in nutrition and holistic wellness, invites readers on a journey that transcends the boundaries of traditional cookbooks.

The odyssey begins with Becky's personal quest for a deeper understanding of the intricate relationship between food and well-being. It's not just a collection of recipes; it's a story that unfolds in the kitchen, where ingredients become characters, and each dish has a tale to tell.

As Becky shares her expertise, readers are guided through a rich tapestry of flavors, textures, and culinary techniques. The narrative isn't confined to the realm of cooking; it's a celebration of the artistry involved in crafting meals that nourish not only the body but also the soul.

Becky Mathew-Smith's Culinary Odyssey is an exploration of whole foods, mindful ingredients, and the joy of savoring each moment. It's an intimate conversation with food, a dance of flavors that mirrors the rhythm of life itself. The odyssey encompasses the nuances of meal planning, the art of balancing nutritional considerations, and the sheer delight of creating dishes that resonate with both palate and heart.

In this culinary narrative, Becky's wisdom becomes a guiding light, offering not just recipes but a holistic approach to wellness. The pages come alive with anecdotes, tips, and a genuine passion for the alchemy that happens in the kitchen. From breakfasts that greet the day with warmth to dinners that bring loved ones together, Becky's odyssey is an invitation to embrace the culinary arts as a form of self-expression and well-being.

As readers embark on Becky Mathew-Smith's Culinary Odyssey, they're not just learning how to cook; they're stepping into a world where every meal is a chapter, and every bite tells a story of vitality, health, and the sheer pleasure of eating well. The odyssey isn't just about reaching a destination; it's about savoring the journey and relishing the flavors along the way.

What is Nickel Allergy?

A common skin allergy that appears as a rash after exposure to anything containing nickel such as jewelry, cell phones, eyeglasses, etc.

Nickel allergy affects about 10% of the people in the US. The rash often becomes evident when you get your ears pierced. In some people, it is causes headaches and other problems. There is no cure for nickel allergy.

Nickel allergy is something that some of us acquire after we are born. The most common underlying event is ear piercing. It is much more common in women than men. This may be because women are more likely to wear jewelry or have piercings.

SYMPTOMS AND CAUSES OF NICKEL ALLERGY

Nickel allergy is a common hypersensitivity reaction to nickel, a metal widely used in various everyday items such as jewelry, clothing fasteners, and electronic devices. While not everyone develops an allergy to nickel, those who do may experience a range of symptoms, and understanding the causes is crucial for effective management.

Symptoms of Nickel Allergy:

Skin Rash:

- A red, itchy rash, often known as contact dermatitis, is a hallmark symptom. This rash may appear where nickel-containing items encounter the skin.

Blistering or Eczema:

- In some cases, prolonged exposure to nickel can lead to the development of blisters or eczema, characterized by inflamed, irritated skin.

Swelling and Redness:

- The affected area may exhibit swelling and redness, contributing to discomfort and a noticeable change in skin appearance.

Dry or Cracked Skin:

- Nickel allergy can lead to dryness and cracking of the skin, particularly in areas where there is frequent contact with nickel-containing items.

Inflammation and Soreness:

- Inflammation and soreness may accompany the rash, intensifying the discomfort experienced by individuals with nickel allergy.

Localized Symptoms:

- Symptoms are often localized to the specific area of contact with nickel, but in severe cases, they can spread to other parts of the body.

Causes of Nickel Allergy:

Genetic Predisposition:

- Some individuals may have a genetic predisposition to nickel allergy, making them more susceptible to developing an immune response when exposed to this metal.

Repeated Exposure:

- Prolonged or repeated exposure to items containing nickel is a significant factor. This includes jewelry, clothing accessories, and tools, as well as items like eyeglass frames or cell phones.

Body Piercings:

- Nickel is commonly found in certain alloys used in body piercings. Pierced areas may be particularly prone to developing nickel allergy symptoms.

Occupational Exposure:

- Certain occupations, such as those involving metalworking or nickel refining, may increase the risk of nickel exposure and subsequent allergy development.

Dental Work:

- Dental work, especially with nickel-containing alloys, can be a source of exposure for some individuals. It's essential to communicate any known allergies to dental professionals.

Dietary Nickel:

- While less common, some individuals may develop nickel allergy symptoms from dietary sources. Certain foods, such as nuts, chocolate, and some vegetables, contain trace amounts of nickel.

Understanding the symptoms and causes of nickel allergy is crucial for both prevention and effective management. Individuals experiencing persistent skin issues or suspecting a nickel allergy should seek medical advice for proper diagnosis and guidance on minimizing exposure to nickel-containing items. Nickel allergy management often involves lifestyle adjustments and, in severe cases, may include medical interventions such as topical or oral corticosteroids.

Nickel Allergy and Dyshidrotic Eczema: Unravelling The Connection

Nickel allergy and dyshidrotic eczema are two distinct conditions, yet their intersection sheds light on a complex relationship between environmental triggers and skin health. Understanding the link between these two can be pivotal for individuals grappling with skin issues and seeking effective management strategies.

Nickel Allergy:

Nickel allergy is a hypersensitivity reaction to nickel, a metal commonly found in various everyday items, including jewelry, clothing fasteners, and electronic devices. When an individual with a nickel allergy comes into contact with nickel, their immune system reacts, leading to a range of skin symptoms such as redness, itching, blistering, and inflammation.

Dyshidrotic Eczema: Exploring The Condition

Dyshidrotic eczema, also known as pompholyx eczema, is a specific form of eczema characterized by small, itchy blisters that typically appear on the hands and feet. The exact cause of dyshidrotic eczema is not fully understood, but it is believed to involve a combination of genetic and environmental factors.

The Intersection: Nickel And Dyshidrotic Eczema

Nickel as a Trigger:

- Nickel is recognized as a potential trigger for dyshidrotic eczema in individuals with a nickel allergy. When these individuals come into contact with nickel, it can exacerbate or even initiate the blistering and itching characteristic of dyshidrotic eczema.

Location of Eruptions:

- Dyshidrotic eczema eruptions often occur on the palms of the hands and soles of the feet. This is consistent with areas where nickel-containing items, such as jewelry or metal fasteners, commonly encounter the skin.

Prolonged Exposure:

- Individuals with a nickel allergy who have prolonged or repeated exposure to nickel may be at an increased risk of developing or worsening dyshidrotic eczema symptoms.

Management and Prevention Strategies:

Avoidance of Nickel:

- The primary strategy for managing the connection between nickel allergy and dyshidrotic eczema involves avoiding direct contact with nickel-containing items. This may include choosing nickel-free jewelry, opting for hypoallergenic clothing fasteners, and being mindful of everyday items that may contain nickel.

Topical Treatments:

- For dyshidrotic eczema symptoms, topical treatments such as corticosteroid creams or ointments may be recommended to alleviate inflammation and itching.

Moisturization:

- Keeping the skin well-moisturized can help manage eczema symptoms. Moisturizers with minimal or no nickel content are preferable.

Consultation with Healthcare Professionals:

- Individuals experiencing persistent or worsening symptoms should seek guidance from healthcare professionals. Dermatologists can provide accurate diagnosis, recommend appropriate treatments, and offer personalized strategies for minimizing nickel exposure.

While nickel allergy and dyshidrotic eczema are distinct entities, their connection emphasizes the intricate relationship between environmental triggers and skin health. Awareness, avoidance, and appropriate medical intervention play crucial roles in managing these conditions effectively, offering relief to those navigating the complexities of nickel-related skin reactions and eczema symptoms.

Nickel Allergy and Irritable Bowel Syndrome (IBS): Unveiling the Interplay

The intricate relationship between nickel allergy and irritable bowel syndrome (IBS) unveils a fascinating interplay between immune responses and gastrointestinal health. While seemingly disparate, these conditions share underlying complexities that can significantly impact an individual's well-being.

Nickel Allergy: A Dermatological Prelude

Nickel allergy, a hypersensitivity reaction to nickel exposure, primarily manifests in dermatological symptoms such as skin rashes, redness, and itching. Commonly triggered by contact with nickel-containing items like jewelry, clothing fasteners, and everyday objects, this immune response is well-documented in the realm of dermatology.

Irritable Bowel Syndrome (IBS): A Gastrointestinal Challenge

In contrast, IBS is a functional gastrointestinal disorder characterized by symptoms such as abdominal pain, bloating, altered bowel habits, and discomfort. The exact cause of IBS is multifactorial and may involve factors such as gut hypersensitivity, altered motility, and the gut-brain axis.

The Interconnected Web: Nickel and Gastrointestinal Impact

Dietary Nickel:

- Nickel, beyond its role in dermatological reactions, can also play a role in gastrointestinal health. Certain foods, especially those rich in nickel, may contribute to dietary nickel exposure. For individuals sensitive to nickel, this can be a factor in triggering or exacerbating gastrointestinal symptoms.

Nickel in Foods:

- Foods such as legumes, nuts, chocolate, and certain vegetables contain varying levels of nickel. For those with both nickel allergy and IBS, managing dietary nickel intake becomes crucial in addressing potential gastrointestinal discomfort.

Immune Response and Gut Health:

- The immune response triggered by nickel allergy may extend beyond the skin to affect the gastrointestinal system. In some individuals, this immune reactivity could contribute to or exacerbate existing gut-related symptoms, potentially influencing the development or severity of IBS.

Management Strategies:

Dietary Modifications:

- For individuals with both nickel allergy and IBS, adopting a low-nickel diet may be beneficial. This involves avoiding or minimizing the consumption of foods high in nickel, potentially alleviating both dermatological and gastrointestinal symptoms.

Medical Guidance:

- Seeking medical advice is crucial for accurate diagnosis and tailored management. Dermatologists and gastroenterologists can collaborate to provide comprehensive care, addressing both the dermatological and gastrointestinal aspects of the conditions.

Individualized Approach:

- Recognizing that each person's experience is unique is paramount. Tailoring management strategies to an individual's specific symptoms, triggers, and sensitivities is key to achieving optimal outcomes.

Navigating the Dual Challenge

While nickel allergy and IBS may appear distinct, their interconnectedness illuminates the intricate ways in which immune responses can impact different systems within the body. Understanding this interplay allows for more holistic and personalized approaches to care, emphasizing the importance of collaboration between dermatologists and gastroenterologists to address both dermatological and gastrointestinal aspects effectively.

Nickel Allergy and Endometriosis: Unravelling the Complex Connection

The intersection of nickel allergy and endometriosis introduces a multifaceted interplay between immune responses and reproductive health. While these conditions primarily affect different systems in the body, emerging research suggests a potential link that underscores the intricate nature of autoimmune and inflammatory processes.

Nickel Allergy: A Dermatological Prelude

Nickel allergy, characterized by an immune reaction to nickel exposure, primarily manifests in dermatological symptoms such as skin rashes, itching, and inflammation. Commonly triggered by contact with nickel-containing items like jewelry, clothing fasteners, and everyday objects, this immune response is well-documented in the field of dermatology.

Endometriosis: A Reproductive Challenge

Endometriosis, on the other hand, is a gynecological disorder in which tissue like the lining of the uterus grows outside the uterus. This condition can lead to pelvic pain, fertility challenges, and various reproductive health issues. The exact cause of endometriosis remains complex, involving factors such as genetic predisposition and hormonal imbalances.

Exploring The Connection: Immune Responses and Inflammation

Autoimmune Factors:

- Emerging studies suggest that autoimmune factors may play a role in both nickel allergy and endometriosis. Common immunological mechanisms may contribute to an increased prevalence of autoimmune conditions in individuals with endometriosis.

Inflammatory Responses:

- Both conditions involve inflammatory responses. Nickel allergy triggers an immune-mediated inflammatory reaction, and endometriosis is characterized by chronic inflammation. The shared inflammatory aspect could contribute to the coexistence or exacerbation of symptoms in affected individuals.

Management Strategies: Bridging The Gap

Dietary Modifications:

- For those with nickel allergy and endometriosis, exploring dietary modifications may be beneficial. A low-nickel diet, coupled with anti-inflammatory foods, may help manage symptoms and reduce the impact of inflammatory responses on both conditions.

Integrated Healthcare Approach:

- Collaboration between dermatologists, allergists, and gynecologists is crucial. An integrated healthcare approach can address both the dermatological aspects of nickel allergy and the complex reproductive health challenges posed by endometriosis.

Individualized Care:

- Recognizing the unique experiences of individuals with coexisting nickel allergy and endometriosis is essential. Tailoring treatment plans to the specific symptoms, triggers, and sensitivities of each person allows for a more personalized and effective approach.

Navigating the Complexity

The connection between nickel allergy and endometriosis, while complex, highlights the importance of considering the broader impact of immune responses on different systems within the body. As research progresses, a more nuanced understanding of these interrelationships may pave the way for comprehensive care strategies that address both dermatological and reproductive health concerns. An individualized approach, grounded in collaboration between healthcare professionals, becomes paramount in navigating the intricate landscape of coexisting nickel allergy and endometriosis.

Nickel Allergy and Fibromyalgia: Navigating the Complex Intersection

The connection between nickel allergy and fibromyalgia introduces a layer of complexity, suggesting potential links between immune responses, environmental triggers, and chronic pain conditions. While distinct in their primary manifestations, the coexistence of nickel allergy and fibromyalgia raises intriguing questions about the interplay between immune reactions and widespread pain.

Nickel Allergy: Immune Responses and Dermatological Impact

Nickel allergy stems from an immune reaction to nickel exposure, commonly encountered in everyday items such as jewelry, clothing fasteners, and electronic devices. The immune response leads to dermatological symptoms like skin rashes, itching, and inflammation, with the severity varying among individuals.

Fibromyalgia: Chronic Pain and Widespread Discomfort

Fibromyalgia is characterized by chronic, widespread pain, fatigue, and heightened sensitivity to pain. The exact cause of fibromyalgia remains elusive, but factors such as genetics, infections, and physical or emotional trauma are considered potential contributors to its development.

Exploring Potential Links: Immune Dysfunction and Pain Perception

Immune Dysfunction:

- Emerging research suggests that immune dysfunction may play a role in both nickel allergy and fibromyalgia. Individuals with nickel allergy may experience heightened immune responses, and some studies indicate alterations in immune function in those with fibromyalgia.

Central Sensitization:

- Both conditions involve a phenomenon known as central sensitization, where the nervous system becomes more responsive to pain signals. This shared characteristic could contribute to the overlap of symptoms in individuals affected by both nickel allergy and fibromyalgia.

Management Strategies: Addressing Immune and Pain Dynamics

Avoidance of Nickel Exposure:

- Minimizing exposure to nickel-containing items is crucial for managing nickel allergy symptoms. This may involve choosing hypoallergenic jewelry and being mindful of everyday objects that may contain nickel.

Pain Management:

- Managing chronic pain associated with fibromyalgia is a central aspect of care. This may involve a combination of medications, physical therapy, and lifestyle modifications to enhance overall well-being.

Integrated Healthcare Approach:

- Collaboration between allergists, dermatologists, and rheumatologists is vital. An integrated healthcare approach allows for a comprehensive understanding of both the dermatological impact of nickel allergy and the complex pain dynamics of fibromyalgia.

A Holistic Perspective

The coexistence of nickel allergy and fibromyalgia underscores the intricate relationship between immune responses and chronic pain conditions. While the precise mechanisms linking these conditions are not fully elucidated, a holistic perspective that considers both dermatological and systemic aspects is essential. Individualized care, grounded in collaboration between healthcare professionals, becomes pivotal in navigating the complex intersection of nickel allergy and fibromyalgia, offering comprehensive support for those managing these intertwined health challenges.

CHAPTER TWO
THE SCIENCE BEHIND NICKEL IN OUR DIET

The Role of Nickel In the Environment

Nickel, a versatile transition metal, plays a significant role in various environmental processes and ecosystems. While it is a naturally occurring element, human activities and industrial processes have led to increased nickel concentrations in certain areas, raising environmental concerns. Understanding the multifaceted role of nickel is crucial for managing its impact on ecosystems and human health.

1. Natural Occurrence:

- Nickel is naturally present in the Earth's crust, soil, water, and air. It is an essential component of the Earth's composition, and trace amounts of nickel are found in many rocks, minerals, and organic matter.

2. Geological Processes:

- Geological processes, such as weathering and erosion, contribute to the release of nickel into the environment. This natural mobilization of nickel allows it to enter surface water, sediments, and soils.

3. Biological Functions:

- Nickel is a trace element with biological significance. Some plants, fungi, and bacteria use nickel in enzymes for various physiological processes, including nitrogen fixation in certain plants and methane metabolism in certain microorganisms.

4. Human Activities:

- Human activities, particularly industrial processes such as mining, metallurgy, and the burning of fossil fuels, can release elevated levels of nickel into the environment. This anthropogenic input can contribute to soil and water contamination.

5. Water Contamination:

- Nickel can leach into water sources, leading to potential contamination. Elevated levels of nickel in water may have adverse effects on aquatic ecosystems, affecting the health of aquatic organisms and disrupting ecological balance.

6. Soil Contamination:

- Soil contamination with nickel can occur near industrial sites or areas with extensive agricultural practices. Excessive nickel in soil may impact plant growth and can potentially accumulate in plant tissues, affecting the food chain.

7. Airborne Nickel:

- Certain industrial activities, such as nickel smelting and combustion processes, release nickel particles into the air. Inhalation of airborne nickel particles can pose health risks to humans, as nickel is classified as a potential human carcinogen.

8. Environmental Impact:

- The environmental impact of nickel extends beyond local contamination. Nickel compounds released into the atmosphere can contribute to global environmental issues, including acid rain formation and climate change.

9. Regulatory Measures:

- Due to concerns about the environmental and health impacts of nickel, regulatory measures and environmental standards have been established to monitor and control nickel emissions from industrial sources. These measures aim to mitigate the adverse effects of nickel on ecosystems and human health.

10. Research and Monitoring:

- Ongoing research and environmental monitoring efforts are crucial for assessing the impact of nickel on ecosystems and identifying strategies for sustainable nickel management. This includes studying the bioavailability, mobility, and transformation of nickel in different environmental compartments.

In conclusion, while nickel plays a natural role in the environment, human activities have contributed to its increased presence in certain areas, leading to environmental and health challenges. Sustainable practices, regulatory measures, and ongoing research are essential for managing the role of nickel in the environment and mitigating its potential adverse effects.

How Nickel Enters the Food Chain

Nickel, a naturally occurring element, can enter the food chain through various pathways, both natural and anthropogenic. Understanding these mechanisms is crucial for assessing the potential impact of nickel on human health and ecosystems. Here are key ways in which nickel enters the food chain:

1. **Soil Contamination:**

   - Nickel is present in soil naturally, but human activities, such as industrial processes and the use of nickel-containing fertilizers, can lead to elevated levels of nickel in the soil. Plants absorb nickel from the soil, and the degree of uptake depends on factors such as soil pH and the plant species.

2. **Plant Uptake:**

   - Plants can absorb nickel through their roots from the soil. While not all plants accumulate high levels of nickel, some species, known as hyperaccumulators, can take up and store significant amounts of nickel in their tissues. Common dietary sources of nickel include nuts, legumes, grains, and certain leafy vegetables.

3. **Water Contamination:**

   - Water sources near industrial facilities or areas with nickel mining activities can become contaminated with nickel. Aquatic plants and organisms, as well as fish, may absorb nickel from water, contributing to the nickel content in the aquatic food chain.

4. **Atmospheric Deposition:**

   - Nickel particles released into the air from industrial processes, combustion, or natural sources can settle on the soil and water surfaces through atmospheric deposition. Once deposited, nickel can enter the soil and water, making it available for uptake by plants and, subsequently, entering the food chain.

5. Bioaccumulation:

- In the food chain, nickel can undergo a process called bioaccumulation, where organisms at lower trophic levels absorb and retain nickel, and this concentration increases as it moves up the food chain. Predatory organisms at higher trophic levels may accumulate higher concentrations of nickel due to the cumulative effect.

6. Animal Consumption:

- Animals, including livestock and seafood, can contribute to nickel transfer in the food chain. Animals may ingest nickel directly from contaminated water, soil, or plants. Additionally, predators that consume other animals with accumulated nickel contribute to the transfer of nickel through the food web.

7. Food Processing:

- Food processing and cooking methods can also influence the nickel content in the final food products. Certain materials used in food processing equipment may contain nickel, and acidic or high-temperature conditions during food preparation can facilitate the release of nickel into the food.

8. Human Activities:

- Human activities, such as the use of nickel-plated cookware and utensils, can introduce nickel into food during cooking and food preparation. Dietary choices, including the consumption of nickel-rich foods and beverages, contribute to the overall nickel intake.

9. Occupational Exposure:

- Workers involved in nickel-related industries may be exposed to higher levels of nickel, and this occupational exposure can extend to their clothing, skin, and hair. Contaminated clothing or personal items may introduce nickel into the home environment and, subsequently, the food chain.

Understanding these pathways of nickel entry into the food chain is essential for monitoring and managing nickel exposure. Regulations, agricultural practices, and awareness of sources contributing to nickel contamination can help mitigate potential health and environmental risks associated with elevated nickel levels in the food chain.

Bioavailability of Nickel In Foods: Unravelling Nutritional Dynamics

The bioavailability of nickel in foods refers to the extent to which nickel is absorbed and utilized by the body after ingestion. While nickel is not considered an essential nutrient, understanding its bioavailability is crucial due to its presence in various food sources and potential health implications. The bioavailability of nickel is influenced by factors such as the form of nickel, dietary composition, and individual characteristics.

Forms of Nickel:

Inorganic Nickel:

- Inorganic nickel, the predominant form found in foods, includes nickel salts and compounds. This form of nickel is generally less bioavailable than organic forms.

Organic Nickel:

- Organic nickel, found in certain plants and microorganisms, is considered more bioavailable. It is often associated with specific enzymes and proteins and may play a role in biological processes in those organisms.

Factors Influencing Bioavailability:

Dietary Composition:

- The composition of the diet plays a significant role. Certain dietary components, such as vitamin C, may enhance the absorption of nickel, while dietary fibers and some minerals, like calcium and iron, can inhibit absorption.

Form of Nickel:

- The chemical form of nickel affects its bioavailability. Soluble forms of nickel are generally more readily absorbed than insoluble forms. Food processing methods can also influence the solubility of nickel in foods.

Gastrointestinal Conditions:

- The pH and conditions of the gastrointestinal tract impact nickel absorption. Changes in gastric acidity can influence the solubility of nickel, affecting its absorption in the stomach and intestines.

Individual Characteristics:

- Factors such as age, genetics, and individual health status influence nickel bioavailability. Infants and children may absorb more nickel than adults, and individuals with certain health conditions or genetic variations may experience altered nickel absorption.

Dietary Sources of Nickel:

Plant-Based Foods:

- Nickel is commonly found in plant-based foods, including nuts, seeds, grains, legumes, and leafy vegetables. The bioavailability of nickel from plant sources can vary depending on factors such as soil composition and plant species.

Animal-Based Foods:

- Animal-based foods, including meat, poultry, and fish, may contain nickel, although generally at lower levels than plant-based sources. The bioavailability of nickel from animal sources is influenced by the animal's diet.

Health Implications:
Allergic Reactions:

- Individuals with nickel allergy may experience allergic reactions upon exposure. While dietary nickel does not usually cause allergic reactions, those with nickel sensitivity may need to manage their intake to avoid triggering symptoms.

Chronic Exposure:

- Chronic exposure to elevated levels of nickel, particularly through occupational settings or contaminated environments, can lead to adverse health effects. Monitoring and managing nickel exposure become crucial in such scenarios.

Regulatory Standards:
Maximum Tolerable Intake:

- Regulatory bodies, such as health agencies, establish maximum tolerable intake levels for nickel to protect against adverse health effects. These standards consider the potential risks associated with chronic exposure.

Research and Future Considerations:
Nutritional Studies:

- Ongoing research explores the nutritional dynamics of nickel, aiming to enhance our understanding of its bioavailability, metabolism, and potential health effects.

Public Health Strategies:

- Public health strategies may involve raising awareness of nickel content in foods, implementing dietary guidelines, and promoting balanced nutrition to manage nickel exposure.

In conclusion, while nickel is not an essential nutrient, its bioavailability in foods is a complex interplay of various factors. Understanding these dynamics is essential for assessing potential health risks, especially in individuals with nickel sensitivity, and for informing public health strategies to manage nickel exposure. Continued research will contribute to a more comprehensive understanding of the nutritional and health implications of dietary nickel.

CHAPTER THREE
THE LOW-NICKEL LANDSCAPE

Holistic Insights into The Low-Nickel Lifestyle

It offers a profound and comprehensive discussion, transcending the conventional boundaries of dietary guidance to explore the interconnected facets of health, nutrition, and mindful living. This chapter serves as a beacon for those seeking a more profound understanding of the low-nickel lifestyle.

Understanding the Holistic Approach:

1. Mind-Body Connection:

- The chapter delves into the intricate relationship between mental and physical well-being. It underscores the idea that holistic health involves nourishing not only the body but also fostering a positive and mindful mental state.

2. Nutritional Considerations:

- Beyond the traditional focus on nickel content, the discussion expands to encompass broader nutritional considerations. Readers gain insights into the importance of balanced nutrition, emphasizing the role of vitamins, minerals, and macronutrients in supporting overall health.

3. Lifestyle Harmony:

- Holistic living extends beyond meal choices. The chapter explores lifestyle factors such as sleep, stress management, and physical activity. It advocates for a harmonious lifestyle that complements dietary choices, promoting a holistic sense of well-being.

Embracing Mindful Living:

1. Intentional Eating:

- Becky Mathew-Smith encourages readers to approach their meals with intention. Mindful eating is discussed as a practice that goes beyond nutritional benefits, emphasizing the importance of savoring each bite and cultivating a deeper appreciation for the food on one's plate.

2. Joyful Nourishment:

- The chapter introduces the concept of joyful nourishment, highlighting that food is not merely sustenance but a source of pleasure and connection. Readers are prompted to find joy in their culinary experiences, fostering a positive relationship with the act of eating.

Integrating Holistic Insights into Daily Life:

1. Mealtime Rituals:

- Practical tips are provided for incorporating holistic insights into daily life. Mealtime rituals, such as mindful cooking practices and creating a serene eating environment, are explored as ways to enhance the overall dining experience.

2. Balancing Act:

- The discussion emphasizes the delicate balance required in navigating the low-nickel lifestyle. It addresses the need for flexibility, encouraging readers to find equilibrium between dietary restrictions and the joy of varied and flavorful meals.

The Holistic Lifestyle as A Journey:

1. Long-Term Wellness:

- Holistic living is positioned as a journey rather than a destination. Readers are encouraged to view the low-nickel lifestyle as a long-term commitment to overall wellness, understanding that it encompasses both dietary choices and lifestyle practices.

2. Empowerment through Knowledge:

- The chapter concludes by empowering readers with knowledge. By understanding the holistic approach to the low-nickel lifestyle, individuals are better equipped to make informed choices, fostering a sense of empowerment and control over their well-being.

"Holistic Insights into the Low-Nickel Lifestyle" goes beyond the dietary restrictions typically associated with nickel management, offering a profound exploration of the interconnected elements that contribute to a truly holistic sense of health and well-being. It invites readers to embark on a transformative journey where mindful living and intentional choices become integral components of a flourishing, low-nickel lifestyle.

Dietary Intricacies Unveiled: Navigating The Complex Web of Nutritional Dynamics

Dietary intricacies represent the multifaceted and interwoven complexities that define our relationship with food and its profound impact on our health. Unveiling these intricacies involves exploring a spectrum of factors, from the nutritional composition of foods to individual dietary choices and their far-reaching implications. Let's delve into the various dimensions that make up the rich tapestry of dietary intricacies.

1. Nutritional Composition: The Foundation of Dietary Intricacies

a. Macronutrients:

- The primary building blocks of our diet, macronutrients—carbohydrates, proteins, and fats— form the cornerstone of our nutritional intake. Balancing these essential elements is critical for energy production, cellular function, and overall metabolic health.

b. Micronutrients:

- Delving deeper, micronutrients such as vitamins and minerals play a pivotal role in supporting specific physiological functions. From vitamin C's immune-boosting properties to the bone-strengthening effects of calcium, the intricacies lie in understanding the nuanced impact of each micronutrient.

2. Dietary Patterns: Unravelling The Tapestry of Eating Habits

a. Cultural Influences:

- Dietary intricacies are profoundly shaped by cultural influences, encompassing traditions, culinary practices, and regional food availability. Exploring these cultural nuances provides insights into the diversity of dietary patterns worldwide.

b. Dietary Trends:

- Modern dietary trends, from plant-based lifestyles to intermittent fasting, add layers of complexity. Understanding the rationale behind these trends and their potential impacts on health unveils the dynamic nature of dietary choices.

3. Bioavailability and Food Processing: The Metamorphosis Of Nutrients

a. Bioavailability Challenges:

- Not all nutrients are created equal in terms of absorption. Factors such as food processing methods, cooking techniques, and the presence of other compounds can influence the bioavailability of nutrients, introducing a layer of intricacy in nutrient absorption.

b. Fortification and Enrichment:

- Responding to nutritional gaps, fortification and enrichment of foods aim to enhance their nutritional value. The careful selection and addition of specific nutrients contribute to the intricate science of crafting nutritionally enhanced products.

4. Individual Variability: The Personalized Symphony Of Dietary Responses

a. Nutrigenomics:

- Nutrigenomics explores the interplay between genetics and nutrition, unveiling how individual genetic variations influence responses to dietary components. This field accentuates the personalized nature of dietary intricacies.

b. Metabolic Diversity:

- Metabolic diversity among individuals results in varied responses to the same foods. Factors such as metabolic rate, insulin sensitivity, and gut microbiota contribute to the intricate web of how our bodies process and utilize nutrients.

5. Dietary Impact On Health: Orchestrating Wellness Or Undermining Well-Being

a. Chronic Diseases:

- Dietary intricacies play a pivotal role in the development and prevention of chronic diseases. From cardiovascular health to metabolic disorders, understanding how dietary choices influence disease pathways is essential for promoting long-term well-being.

b. Mental Health:

- Emerging research underscores the connection between diet and mental health. The intricate relationship between nutritional intake and conditions such as depression and anxiety emphasize the holistic impact of dietary choices on overall wellness.

6. Sustainable Nutrition: Balancing Personal Health And Planetary Well-Being

a. Environmental Impact:

- As dietary choices extend beyond personal health to planetary health, the intricate dance of sustainability comes into focus. Considerations such as food sourcing, agricultural practices, and waste reduction form integral components of sustainable nutrition.

b. Ethical Considerations:

- Dietary intricacies also involve ethical considerations, encompassing issues such as animal welfare, fair trade, and the ecological impact of food production. Balancing personal values with nutritional needs adds layers to the decision-making process.

Navigating The Ever-Evolving Landscape Of Dietary Choices

In essence, dietary intricacies form a rich tapestry woven with threads of nutritional science, cultural diversity, individual variability, and global sustainability. Unveiling these intricacies requires a holistic perspective that recognizes the dynamic interplay of factors influencing our dietary decisions and their profound impact on both personal and planetary well-being. As we navigate this ever-evolving landscape, a nuanced understanding of dietary intricacies empowers individuals to make informed choices that contribute to a harmonious balance between nutrition, health, and the broader ecosystem.

Nutritional Considerations for Vibrant Living: Nourishing Your Body, Mind, and Soul

Embracing vibrant living involves more than just the absence of illness; it's about cultivating a holistic sense of well-being that radiates through every aspect of your life. At the core of this vitality lies a set of nutritional considerations that not only fuel the body but also contribute to mental clarity, emotional balance, and a harmonious connection with the world around you. Let's explore the key nutritional pillars for fostering vibrant living.

1. Wholesome Nutrient-Rich Foods: The Foundation of Vitality

a. Colorful Plant-Based Foods:

- Embrace the vibrant hues of fruits and vegetables, as their diverse colors signify an array of essential nutrients. These plant-based powerhouses provide antioxidants, vitamins, and minerals crucial for cellular health and immune function.

b. Lean Proteins:

- Prioritize lean protein sources such as poultry, fish, legumes, and tofu. Proteins are the building blocks of tissues, supporting muscle health, immune function, and overall vitality.

c. Healthy Fats:

- Incorporate sources of healthy fats, including avocados, nuts, seeds, and olive oil. These fats contribute to brain health, hormone production, and the absorption of fat-soluble vitamins.

2. Balanced Nutrition: Nurturing Mind and Body Harmony

a. Macro and Micro Nutrient Balance:

- Strive for a balanced intake of macronutrients (carbohydrates, proteins, fats) and micronutrients (vitamins, minerals) to support diverse physiological functions. This balance contributes to sustained energy levels and overall well-being.

b. Mindful Eating Practices:

- Cultivate awareness around eating habits. Practice mindful eating, savoring each bite, and paying attention to hunger and fullness cues. Mindful eating fosters a positive relationship with food and enhances digestion.

3. Hydration: Quenching the Body's Thirst for Vitality

a. Water as a Lifeforce:

- Hydration is fundamental to vibrant living. Water supports digestion, nutrient transport, and temperature regulation. Aim for adequate water intake throughout the day, adjusting based on individual needs and activity levels.

b. Herbal Teas and Infusions:

- Explore herbal teas and infusions for added hydration and potential health benefits. Teas like green tea or herbal blends can provide antioxidants and promote a sense of calm.

4. Functional Foods: Elevating Health Beyond Basics

a. Superfoods:

- Integrate nutrient-dense superfoods into your diet, such as kale, berries, chia seeds, and turmeric. These foods pack a nutritional punch, offering a range of health-promoting compounds.

b. Fermented Foods:

- Enhance gut health with fermented foods like yogurt, kefir, sauerkraut, and kimchi. A healthy gut microbiome is linked to improved digestion, immune function, and mental well-being.

5. Mind-Body Connection: Nourishing the Soul
a. Nutrients for Brain Health:

- Prioritize nutrients that support brain health, including omega-3 fatty acids (found in fatty fish and flaxseeds) and antioxidants from colorful fruits and vegetables. These nutrients contribute to cognitive function and emotional well-being.

b. Adaptogens:

- Explore adaptogenic herbs like ashwagandha and holy basil, which are believed to support the body's stress response. These herbs may help promote mental resilience and balance.

6. Personalized Nutrition: Tailoring to your Unique Needs
a. Individual Variability:

- Recognize that nutritional needs vary among individuals. Factors such as age, gender, activity level, and health conditions influence dietary requirements. Personalize your nutrition to align with your unique lifestyle and goals.

b. Consultation with Professionals:

- Consider consulting with nutrition professionals or healthcare providers to create a personalized nutrition plan. Their expertise can guide you in optimizing your dietary choices for vibrant living.

7. Sustainable Eating: Nurturing the Planet and Future Generations

a. Ethical Food Choices:

- Make choices that align with your values, considering ethical and sustainable food practices. Support local and eco-friendly options, minimizing your environmental impact.

b. Plant-Centric Diets:

- Explore plant-centric diets, such as vegetarianism or flexitarianism, which can be both nutritionally sound and environmentally conscious. Balancing plant-based foods with mindful choices contributes to sustainable living.

8. Physical Activity: The Synergy of Nutrition and Exercise

a. Pre- and Post-Workout Nutrition:

- Align your nutritional choices with your physical activity. Consider pre-workout snacks for energy and post-workout meals to replenish nutrients. A balanced approach supports exercise performance and recovery.

b. Hydration during Exercise:

- During physical activity, prioritize hydration. Water helps regulate body temperature and ensures optimal muscle function. Tailor your fluid intake based on the intensity and duration of your exercise routine.

9. Culinary Exploration: Flavorful Journeys to Nourishment

a. Culinary Creativity:

- Infuse excitement into your meals by exploring diverse cuisines and cooking techniques. Embrace herbs, spices, and aromatic ingredients to elevate both the nutritional and sensory aspects of your food.

b. Cooking at Home:

- Engage in home cooking whenever possible. This allows you to control ingredients, experiment with nutrient-dense recipes, and foster a deeper connection with the food you consume.

10. Social and Emotional Nourishment: Beyond The Plate

a. Shared Meals:

- Foster social connections through shared meals. Dining with friends and family not only enhances the enjoyment of food but also contributes to emotional well-being.

b. Mindful Eating Practices:

- Practice mindful eating not just as an individual endeavor but also as a shared experience. Encourage presence and gratitude during meals, cultivating a positive and nourishing environment.

11. Continuous Learning: Empowering Nutritional Literacy

a. Stay Informed:

- Nutrition science evolves, so stay informed about the latest research and developments. Understanding nutritional information empowers you to make informed choices aligned with your well-being goals.

b. Consultation with Experts:

- If navigating the complexities of nutrition feels overwhelming, seek guidance from registered dietitians, nutritionists, or healthcare professionals. Their expertise provides personalized insights tailored to your unique needs.

12. Reflective Practices: Your Personal Wellness Journey

a. Journaling:

- Maintain a nutrition journal to track your dietary choices, energy levels, and emotional responses to food. Reflecting on your eating patterns can reveal insights into your overall well-being.

b. Intuitive Eating:

- Embrace intuitive eating, tuning into your body's signals of hunger and fullness. Listen to your body's cues, allowing for a more harmonious relationship with food and enhanced self-awareness.

Sustaining the Tapestry of Vibrant Living

In weaving the intricate fabric of vibrant living, these nutritional considerations serve as threads that intertwine to create a resilient and colorful tapestry. Nourishing your body, mind, and soul requires a holistic approach that extends beyond the plate. By embracing diverse, nutrient-rich foods, personalizing your nutritional choices, and considering the broader impact on the planet, you contribute to a life filled with vitality, joy, and a profound sense of well-being. As you embark on this ongoing journey, may each bite and mindful choice bring you closer to the vibrant and fulfilling life you deserve.

Lifestyle Adjustments for Thriving

Embracing a low-nickel diet is not just a shift in eating habits; it's a holistic lifestyle adjustment aimed at thriving despite the challenges of nickel allergy. The journey toward optimal well-being involves intentional changes that extend beyond the kitchen, intertwining nutritional considerations with broader aspects of daily life. Let's explore how lifestyle adjustments connect with the subject matter of a "Low-Nickel Diet Cookbook for Beginners."

1. Mindful Culinary Exploration:

Connection:

- Lifestyle adjustments for thriving in the context of a low-nickel diet involve a mindful exploration of culinary choices. This includes not only learning to identify low-nickel ingredients but also discovering new cooking methods and flavor profiles that align with dietary restrictions.

Example:

- A lifestyle adjustment can be seen in the intentional exploration of the cookbook's recipes. Beginners on a low-nickel diet engage in a culinary journey, experimenting with fresh, low-nickel ingredients and incorporating flavorful alternatives that cater to their dietary needs.

2. Social Connection through Shared Meals:

Connection:

- Lifestyle adjustments emphasize the importance of maintaining social connections, even in the context of dietary restrictions. Shared meals with friends and family become a focal point, creating an environment that supports both social well-being and adherence to a low-nickel diet.

Example:

- The low-nickel diet cookbook can serve as a tool for fostering social connections. By sharing meals prepared from the cookbook, individuals not only adhere to their dietary requirements but also involve loved ones in their culinary journey, turning it into a shared and enjoyable experience.

3. Personalized Nutrition for Optimal Health:

Connection:

- Lifestyle adjustments involve tailoring nutritional choices to individual needs. For those on a low-nickel diet, this means understanding not only the nickel content of foods but also personalizing meals to meet nutritional requirements and support overall health.

Example:

- Individuals following the low-nickel diet are empowered to make informed choices using the cookbook's guidance. Adjusting their lifestyle to incorporate personalized nutrition ensures that their meals not only adhere to dietary restrictions but also contribute to their overall well-being.

4. Reflective Practices for Dietary Awareness:

Connection:

- Lifestyle adjustments encourage reflective practices, such as keeping a food journal, to enhance dietary awareness. For those on a low-nickel diet, this awareness is crucial for making conscious choices that align with their health goals.

Example:

- The cookbook can be integrated into reflective practices, with users documenting their experiences and reactions to various recipes. This not only deepens their understanding of how their bodies respond to specific foods but also facilitates a mindful and intentional approach to the low-nickel lifestyle.

5. Holistic Well-being Beyond the Plate:

Connection:

- Lifestyle adjustments extend beyond dietary considerations, aiming for holistic well-being. Integrating practices that promote mental, emotional, and physical health ensures a comprehensive approach to thriving on a low-nickel diet.

Example:

- Incorporating stress-reducing activities, regular exercise, and mindfulness practices aligns with the broader concept of lifestyle adjustments. This holistic approach, coupled with the cookbook's recipes, contributes to an overall sense of well-being for individuals managing a low-nickel diet.

In the realm of a "Low-Nickel Diet Cookbook for Beginners," lifestyle adjustments form an integral part of the journey toward thriving despite dietary restrictions. The cookbook serves not only as a source of delicious and low-nickel recipes but also as a guide for individuals adjusting their lifestyles to embrace the nuances of a low-nickel diet.

Through mindful culinary exploration, social connection, personalized nutrition, reflective practices, and a holistic well-being focus, the cookbook becomes a comprehensive lifestyle adjustment guide, empowering beginners to navigate and thrive on their low-nickel journey.

CHAPTER FOUR
THE NICKEL ODYSSEY BEGINS

Breakfasts Beyond Boundaries

In the immersive journey through the "Low Nickel Diet Cookbook for Beginners," Chapter 4, titled "The Nickel Odyssey Begins," emerges as a pivotal section that delves into the heart of the cookbook. The sub-chapter, "Breakfasts Beyond Boundaries," serves as a vibrant exploration of the morning meal, introducing beginners to a world of delicious possibilities while adhering to the principles of a low-nickel diet.

Discussion:

Diverse Breakfast Options:

- "Breakfasts Beyond Boundaries" opens the door to a diverse array of breakfast options carefully crafted for those navigating a low-nickel lifestyle. From energizing and nutrient-packed choices to palate-pleasing delights, this sub-chapter aims to redefine breakfast for individuals with nickel sensitivity.

Creative Recipe Development:

- The breakfast recipes featured in this sub-chapter showcase the creativity of the cookbook's approach. Each recipe is a testament to the innovation and ingenuity involved in adapting traditional breakfast favorites to align with low-nickel guidelines. Expect to find a variety of dishes that cater to different tastes and dietary preferences.

Balancing Nutrition and Flavor:

- One of the key highlights of "Breakfasts Beyond Boundaries" is the emphasis on balancing nutrition and flavor. The recipes are meticulously designed to provide essential nutrients while ensuring a delightful culinary experience. This sub-chapter sets the tone for a day that begins with nourishment and enjoyment.

Accessibility for Beginners:

- Recognizing that beginners may feel overwhelmed by the prospect of a low-nickel diet, "Breakfasts Beyond Boundaries" aims to make the transition accessible and enjoyable. The recipes are beginner-friendly, featuring clear instructions, easily sourced ingredients, and practical tips for seamless preparation.

Incorporating Fresh Ingredients:

- The sub-chapter highlights the importance of incorporating fresh, whole ingredients into breakfast recipes. From vibrant fruits to nutrient-dense grains, each recipe encourages a focus on wholesome elements that not only align with low-nickel guidelines but also contribute to overall well-being.

Mindful Eating Practices:

- Beyond the recipes themselves, "Breakfasts Beyond Boundaries" introduces the concept of mindful eating. The sub-chapter encourages readers to savor each bite, appreciate the flavors, and be present in the moment. This mindful approach fosters a positive relationship with food and enhances the overall breakfast experience.

Setting the Tone for the Day:

- Breakfast is often considered the foundation of a day's nourishment, and this sub-chapter recognizes its significance. By providing a range of options that are not only low in nickel but also delicious and satisfying, "Breakfasts Beyond Boundaries" sets a positive tone for the entire day, empowering beginners to approach their low-nickel journey with enthusiasm.

"Breakfasts Beyond Boundaries" in Chapter 4 of the "Low Nickel Diet Cookbook for Beginners" goes beyond being a collection of recipes. It is a thoughtful and engaging exploration of the breakfast experience within the context of a low-nickel diet. Through innovative recipes, accessibility for beginners, and a focus on mindful nutrition, this sub-chapter becomes a valuable resource, inviting individuals to embrace a new chapter in their culinary odyssey.

Quinoa Breakfast Bowl
Ingredients:

- 1/2 cup quinoa, rinsed
- 1 cup almond milk (or any preferred milk)
- 1/2 teaspoon vanilla extract
- 1 tablespoon maple syrup
- 1/2 cup mixed berries (strawberries, blueberries, raspberries)
- 1 medium banana, sliced
- 1 tablespoon chia seeds
- 1 tablespoon chopped nuts (almonds, walnuts, or your choice)
- Greek yogurt for topping (optional)

Instructions:

1. **Prepare Quinoa:**

   - Rinse quinoa thoroughly under cold water.
   - In a saucepan, combine quinoa and almond milk.
   - Bring to a boil, then reduce heat to low, cover, and simmer for 15-20 minutes or until quinoa is cooked and the liquid is absorbed.
   - Remove from heat and let it sit covered for an additional 5 minutes.
   - Fluff the quinoa with a fork.

2. **Sweeten and Flavor:**

    - Stir in vanilla extract and maple syrup into the cooked quinoa.

3. **Assemble the Bowl:**

    - Divide the sweetened quinoa into serving bowls.

4. **Add Fresh Fruits:**

    - Top each bowl with a generous portion of mixed berries and banana slices.

5. **Enhance with Superfoods:**

    - Sprinkle chia seeds and chopped nuts over the fruit layer.

6. **Optional Greek Yogurt Topping:**

    - If desired, add a dollop of Greek yogurt on top for extra creaminess and protein.

7. **Serve and Enjoy:**

    - Serve the Quinoa Breakfast Bowl immediately while it's warm.

Nutritional Values (per serving):

- Calories: 350 kcal

- Protein: 10g

- Carbohydrates: 60g

- Dietary Fiber: 8g

- Sugars: 16g

- Fat: 8g

- Saturated Fat: 1g

- Cholesterol: 0mg

- Sodium: 120mg

- Calcium: 300mg

- Iron: 3mg

Note: Nutritional values are approximate and may vary based on specific ingredients and portion sizes.

Why it's Nutrient-Rich: This Quinoa Breakfast Bowl is a nutrient-rich powerhouse. Quinoa provides a complete protein source, and the addition of nuts and chia seeds contributes healthy fats and additional protein. Berries bring antioxidants and vitamins, while the banana adds natural sweetness and potassium. This breakfast bowl is not only delicious but also a well-balanced and satisfying start to your day. Adjust ingredients and portion sizes according to your dietary preferences and energy needs.

Sunrise Smoothie Delight Recipes

1. Tropical Citrus Bliss:

Ingredients:

- 1 cup frozen mango chunks
- 1/2 cup frozen pineapple chunks
- 1/2 orange, peeled
- 1/2 banana
- 1/2 cup Greek yogurt
- 1 tablespoon chia seeds
- 1 cup coconut water

Instructions:

1. Place all ingredients in a blender.
2. Blend until smooth and creamy.
3. Pour into a glass and enjoy!

Nutritional Values (per serving):

- Calories: 280 kcal
- Protein: 12g
- Carbohydrates: 45g
- Dietary Fiber: 8g
- Sugars: 28g
- Fat: 8g
- Saturated Fat: 3g
- Cholesterol: 0mg
- Sodium: 80mg

2. Berry Burst Delight:

Ingredients:

- 1/2 cup frozen strawberries
- 1/2 cup frozen blueberries
- 1/2 cup frozen raspberries
- 1/2 banana
- 1/2 cup plain yogurt
- 1 tablespoon flaxseeds
- 1 cup almond milk

Instructions:

1. Combine all ingredients in a blender.
2. Blend until smooth.
3. Pour into a glass and savor the berry goodness!

Nutritional Values (per serving):

- Calories: 220 kcal
- Protein: 9g
- Carbohydrates: 38g
- Dietary Fiber: 10g
- Sugars: 22g
- Fat: 6g
- Saturated Fat: 1g
- Cholesterol: 0mg
- Sodium: 90mg

3. Green Goddess Energizer:

Ingredients:

- 1 cup spinach leaves
- 1/2 cup kale leaves, stems removed
- 1/2 green apple, cored
- 1/2 cucumber, peeled
- 1/2 lemon, peeled
- 1/2 banana
- 1 tablespoon hemp seeds
- 1 cup coconut water

Instructions:

1. Add all ingredients to a blender.
2. Blend until smooth and vibrant.
3. Pour into a glass and relish the green goodness!

Nutritional Values (per serving):

- Calories: 210 kcal
- Protein: 9g
- Carbohydrates: 40g
- Dietary Fiber: 9g
- Sugars: 20g
- Fat: 6g
- Saturated Fat: 1g
- Cholesterol: 0mg
- Sodium: 120mg

4. Peachy Keen Refresher:

Ingredients:

- 1 cup frozen peaches
- 1/2 cup frozen mango chunks
- 1/2 cup plain yogurt
- 1/2 orange, peeled
- 1/2 banana
- 1 tablespoon chia seeds
- 1 cup water or coconut water

Instructions:

1. Combine all ingredients in a blender.
2. Blend until smooth and peachy.
3. Pour into a glass and enjoy the refreshing taste!

Nutritional Values (per serving):

- Calories: 240 kcal
- Protein: 9g
- Carbohydrates: 46g
- Dietary Fiber: 8g
- Sugars: 32g
- Fat: 6g
- Saturated Fat: 1g
- Cholesterol: 0mg / Sodium: 70mg

5. Creamy Banana-Coconut Dream:

Ingredients:

- 1 large banana
- 1/2 cup coconut milk
- 1/2 cup vanilla yogurt
- 1 tablespoon almond butter
- 1 tablespoon shredded coconut (unsweetened)
- 1/2 teaspoon ground cinnamon
- 1 cup ice cubes

Instructions:

1. Place all ingredients in a blender.
2. Blend until creamy and dreamy.
3. Pour into a glass and experience the tropical delight!

Nutritional Values (per serving):

- Calories: 320 kcal
- Protein: 8g
- Carbohydrates: 45g
- Dietary Fiber: 6g
- Sugars: 28g
- Fat: 14g
- Saturated Fat: 8g
- Cholesterol: 5mg
- Sodium: 60mg

Note: *Nutritional values are approximate and may vary based on specific ingredients and portion sizes.*

Why Sunrise Smoothie Delight is nutrient-rich:

The "Sunrise Smoothie Delight" collection is not just a treat for the taste buds; it's a nutrient-packed symphony designed to nourish your body and support overall well-being. Let's explore why these smoothies are a nutrient-rich addition to your daily routine:

Abundance of Vitamins and Minerals:

- Each "Sunrise Smoothie Delight" is a treasure trove of vitamins and minerals derived from a variety of fruits, vegetables, and superfoods. These nutrients play crucial roles in supporting immune function, promoting healthy skin, and contributing to overall vitality.

Dietary Fiber for Digestive Health:

- The inclusion of fiber-rich ingredients such as fruits, vegetables, and seeds ensures that these smoothies are excellent for digestive health. Fiber aids in maintaining bowel regularity, stabilizing blood sugar levels, and supporting a healthy gut microbiome.

Antioxidant Powerhouse:

- Berries, citrus fruits, and greens featured in the smoothies are packed with antioxidants. These compounds help combat oxidative stress, reduce inflammation, and protect cells from damage, contributing to long-term health and disease prevention.

Protein for Sustained Energy:

- Greek yogurt, almond butter, chia seeds, and flaxseeds contribute to the protein content of the smoothies. Protein is essential for muscle repair, satiety, and sustained energy, making these smoothies a wholesome choice for breakfast or a snack.

Healthy Fats for Brain Health:

- Ingredients like chia seeds, nuts, and coconut milk provide a dose of healthy fats. These fats, including omega-3 fatty acids, are crucial for brain health, supporting cognitive function and overall mental well-being.

Hydration with Coconut Water:

- Coconut water serves as a hydrating base for some of the smoothies. Hydration is fundamental for various bodily functions, and coconut water not only adds a refreshing taste but also provides electrolytes to support optimal hydration.

Adaptogenic Benefits:

- Some smoothies incorporate adaptogenic ingredients like hemp seeds. Adaptogens are believed to help the body adapt to stress, supporting the body's resilience and promoting a sense of balance.

Balanced Macronutrients:

- Each "Sunrise Smoothie Delight" is thoughtfully crafted to provide a balance of macronutrients—carbohydrates, proteins, and fats. This balance ensures that the smoothies offer sustained energy, prevent blood sugar spikes, and keep you feeling satisfied.

Customizable for Dietary Preferences:

- The recipes are versatile and can be adapted to various dietary preferences. Whether you're following a vegetarian, vegan, or dairy-free diet, the smoothies can be customized to suit your individual needs and preferences.

In conclusion, "Sunrise Smoothie Delight" is nutrient-rich due to its diverse and colorful array of ingredients. These smoothies go beyond taste, offering a wholesome combination of vitamins, minerals, fiber, protein, and healthy fats—all contributing to a delicious and nutritionally dense beverage that supports your journey to vibrant health.

Nutty Banana Pancakes Recipes

Ingredients:

- 1 ripe banana, mashed
- 1 cup whole wheat flour
- 1 cup milk (dairy or plant-based)
- 1 egg
- 1/4 cup chopped nuts (walnuts, almonds, or pecans)
- 1 tablespoon honey or maple syrup
- 1 teaspoon baking powder
- 1/2 teaspoon cinnamon
- Pinch of salt
- Butter or oil for cooking

Instructions:

1. In a mixing bowl, combine mashed banana, flour, milk, egg, chopped nuts, honey or maple syrup, baking powder, cinnamon, and salt.
2. Mix until just combined; do not overmix.
3. Heat a skillet or griddle over medium heat and add a small amount of butter or oil.
4. Pour 1/4 cup of batter onto the skillet for each pancake.
5. Cook until bubbles form on the surface, then flip and cook the other side until golden brown.
6. Repeat until all the batter is used.

7. Serve with additional sliced bananas and a drizzle of honey or maple syrup.

Nutritional Values (per serving):

- Calories: 280 kcal

- Protein: 9g

- Carbohydrates: 40g

- Dietary Fiber: 6g

- Sugars: 12g

- Fat: 11g

- Saturated Fat: 2g

- Cholesterol: 45mg

- Sodium: 320mg

2. Almond Flour Nutty Banana Pancakes (Gluten-Free):

Ingredients:

- 1 ripe banana, mashed

- 1 cup almond flour

- 1/2 cup milk (dairy or plant-based)

- 2 eggs

- 1/4 cup chopped almonds

- 1 tablespoon honey or maple syrup

- 1 teaspoon baking powder

- 1/2 teaspoon vanilla extract

- Pinch of salt

- Butter or oil for cooking

Instructions:

1. In a bowl, whisk together mashed banana, almond flour, milk, eggs, chopped almonds, honey or maple syrup, baking powder, vanilla extract, and salt.

2. Heat a skillet over medium heat and add a small amount of butter or oil.

3. Spoon 1/4 cup of batter onto the skillet for each pancake.

4. Cook until the edges set and the bottom is golden, then flip and cook the other side.

5. Repeat until all the batter is used.

6. Top with sliced bananas and an extra drizzle of honey or maple syrup.

Nutritional Values (per serving):

- Calories: 320 kcal
- Protein: 12g
- Carbohydrates: 20g
- Dietary Fiber: 4g
- Sugars: 8g
- Fat: 24g
- Saturated Fat: 2g
- Cholesterol: 95mg
- Sodium: 220mg

3. Peanut Butter Banana Protein Pancakes:

Ingredients:

- 2 ripe bananas, mashed
- 1 cup oats (blended into flour)
- 1/2 cup Greek yogurt
- 2 eggs
- 1/4 cup peanut butter
- 1 tablespoon honey or maple syrup
- 1 teaspoon baking powder
- Pinch of salt
- Butter or oil for cooking

Instructions:

1. In a bowl, mix mashed bananas, oat flour, Greek yogurt, eggs, peanut butter, honey or maple syrup, baking powder, and salt.
2. Heat a skillet over medium heat and add a small amount of butter or oil.
3. Spoon 1/4 cup of batter onto the skillet for each pancake.
4. Cook until bubbles form on the surface, then flip and cook the other side.
5. Repeat until all the batter is used.
6. Serve with an additional dollop of Greek yogurt and a drizzle of honey.

Nutritional Values (per serving):

- Calories: 380 kcal

- Protein: 18g

- Carbohydrates: 40g

- Dietary Fiber: 5g

- Sugars: 14g

- Fat: 18g

- Saturated Fat: 4g

- Cholesterol: 125mg

- Sodium: 320mg

4. Coconut Flour Banana Pancakes (Paleo-Friendly):

Ingredients:

- 2 ripe bananas, mashed

- 1/2 cup coconut flour

- 1/2 cup coconut milk

- 3 eggs

- 1/4 cup shredded coconut

- 1 tablespoon honey or maple syrup

- 1 teaspoon baking powder

- Pinch of salt

- Butter or oil for cooking

Instructions:

1. In a bowl, combine mashed bananas, coconut flour, coconut milk, eggs, shredded coconut, honey or maple syrup, baking powder, and salt.

2. Heat a skillet over medium heat and add a small amount of butter or oil.

3. Spoon 1/4 cup of batter onto the skillet for each pancake.

4. Cook until the edges set and the bottom is golden, then flip and cook the other side.

5. Repeat until all the batter is used.

6. Top with additional shredded coconut and a drizzle of honey.

Nutritional Values (per serving):

- Calories: 290 kcal
- Protein: 8g
- Carbohydrates: 30g
- Dietary Fiber: 8g
- Sugars: 14g
- Fat: 16g
- Saturated Fat: 10g
- Cholesterol: 165mg
- Sodium: 320mg

5. Blueberry Walnut Banana Pancakes:

Ingredients:

- 2 ripe bananas, mashed
- 1 cup whole wheat flour
- 1 cup milk (dairy or plant-based)
- 2 eggs
- 1/2 cup blueberries
- 1/4 cup chopped walnuts
- 1 tablespoon honey or maple syrup
- 1 teaspoon baking powder
- Pinch of salt
- Butter or oil for cooking

Instructions:

1. In a mixing bowl, combine mashed bananas, flour, milk, eggs, blueberries, chopped walnuts, honey or maple syrup, baking powder, and salt.
2. Mix until just combined; do not overmix.
3. Heat a skillet or griddle over medium heat and add a small amount of butter or oil.
4. Pour 1/4 cup of batter onto the skillet for each pancake.
5. Cook until bubbles form on the surface, then flip and cook the other side until golden brown.
6. Repeat until all the batter is used.
7. Serve with extra blueberries and a drizzle of honey or maple syrup.

Nutritional Values (per serving):

- Calories: 340 kcal
- Protein: 12g
- Carbohydrates: 50g
- Dietary Fiber: 6g
- Sugars: 14g
- Fat: 10g
- Saturated Fat: 2g
- Cholesterol: 95mg
- Sodium: 330mg

Why Nutty Banana Pancakes are nutrient-rich:

1. **Natural Sweetness and Fiber from Bananas:**

   - Bananas provide natural sweetness along with dietary fiber, promoting digestive health and providing a natural source of energy.

2. **Protein-Packed:**

   - Incorporating eggs and dairy or plant-based alternatives ensures a good protein content, supporting muscle health, and providing a satiating breakfast.

3. **Healthy Fats from Nuts and Nut Butters:**

   - Chopped nuts and nut butters contribute healthy fats, including omega-3 fatty acids and monounsaturated fats, which are essential for heart health and overall well-being.

4. **Whole Grains for Sustained Energy:**

   - Whole wheat or alternative flours introduce complex carbohydrates, offering sustained energy and keeping blood sugar levels stable.

5. **Versatile and Adaptable:**

   - These recipes are adaptable to various dietary preferences, including gluten-free, paleo, and vegetarian, making them suitable for a wide range of individuals.

6. **Customizable Toppings:**

   - Toppings such as honey, maple syrup, fresh fruits, and yogurt not only enhance flavor but also add additional nutrients and antioxidants.

In summary, Nutty Banana Pancakes are nutrient-rich due to their well-balanced combination of carbohydrates, proteins, healthy fats, and fiber. They provide a delicious and satisfying breakfast option that supports overall health and wellness.

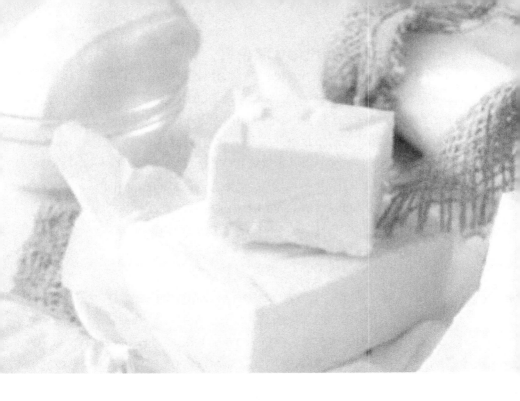

CHAPTER FIVE
LUNCH SYMPHONY

Empowering Midday Meals

In the culinary symphony that is the "Low Nickel Diet Cookbook for Beginners," Chapter 5 unfolds as a harmonious composition entitled "Lunch Symphony." This sub-chapter encapsulates the essence of midday nourishment, providing both beginners and seasoned practitioners of the low-nickel lifestyle with a diverse repertoire of flavorful and nutritious lunch options.

Discussion:

Variety of Lunchtime Delights:

- "Lunch Symphony" introduces a medley of delightful recipes specifically tailored for those navigating a low-nickel diet. From vibrant salads to hearty main courses, this sub-chapter caters to a spectrum of tastes and preferences, ensuring that each meal is a pleasurable and satisfying experience.

Balancing Nutritional Needs:

- Recognizing the importance of balanced nutrition, the recipes within this sub-chapter are thoughtfully crafted to provide essential nutrients while adhering to low-nickel guidelines. Whether you're craving a protein-packed dish or a veggie-centric delight, "Lunch Symphony" empowers individuals to make informed and health-conscious choices.

Innovative Ingredient Pairings:

- Beyond conventional lunch options, this sub-chapter explores innovative ingredient pairings that elevate the low-nickel dining experience. By combining fresh produce, lean proteins, and mindful grains, each recipe becomes a testament to the creativity and versatility inherent in a well-curated low-nickel menu.

Practicality and Accessibility:

- Understanding the demands of modern lifestyles, "Lunch Symphony" prioritizes practicality and accessibility. The recipes are designed to be easily incorporated into daily routines, offering not only a burst of flavor but also a hassle-free approach to preparing nutritious midday meals.

Diversity in Cultural Influences:

- Celebrating the richness of culinary diversity, this sub-chapter draws inspiration from various cultural influences. Whether it's a Mediterranean-inspired quinoa salad or a protein-packed Asian stir-fry, "Lunch Symphony" embraces global flavors, providing a passport to a world of tastes that align with low-nickel requirements.

Mindful Eating Practices:

- Beyond the recipes themselves, "Lunch Symphony" encourages the practice of mindful eating. By savoring each bite, appreciating the textures and flavors, individuals can foster a positive relationship with food. This mindful approach not only enhances the dining experience but also promotes a holistic sense of well-being.

A Comprehensive Midday Guide:

- Serving as a comprehensive midday guide, this sub-chapter extends beyond individual recipes. It equips readers with practical tips on meal planning, portion control, and strategies for navigating lunchtime challenges, ensuring that "Lunch Symphony" becomes an invaluable resource in the daily quest for a balanced and low-nickel diet.

In conclusion, "Lunch Symphony" in Chapter 5 of the "Low Nickel Diet Cookbook for Beginners" transcends the boundaries of a traditional cookbook. It becomes a melodic journey, guiding individuals through the art of crafting empowering midday meals that not only comply with low-nickel restrictions but also elevate the lunchtime experience to a harmonious and healthful crescendo.

Mediterranean Chickpea Salad Recipes

1. Classic Mediterranean Chickpea Salad:

Ingredients:

- 2 cans (15 oz each) chickpeas, drained and rinsed
- 1 cucumber, diced
- 1 cup cherry tomatoes, halved
- 1/2 red onion, finely chopped
- 1/2 cup Kalamata olives, sliced
- 1/2 cup feta cheese, crumbled
- 1/4 cup fresh parsley, chopped
- 1/4 cup extra virgin olive oil
- 2 tablespoons red wine vinegar
- 1 teaspoon dried oregano
- Salt and pepper to taste

Instructions:

1. In a large bowl, combine chickpeas, cucumber, cherry tomatoes, red onion, olives, feta cheese, and parsley.

2. In a small bowl, whisk together olive oil, red wine vinegar, dried oregano, salt, and pepper.

3. Pour the dressing over the salad and toss gently to combine.

4. Refrigerate for at least 30 minutes before serving to allow flavors to meld.

5. Serve chilled and enjoy the classic Mediterranean flavors.

Nutritional Values (per serving):

- Calories: 320 kcal
- Protein: 12g
- Carbohydrates: 32g
- Dietary Fiber: 9g
- Sugars: 5g
- Fat: 18g
- Saturated Fat: 4g
- Cholesterol: 15mg
- Sodium: 560mg

2. Lemon Herb Mediterranean Chickpea Salad:

Ingredients:

- 2 cans (15 oz each) chickpeas, drained and rinsed
- 1 cup English cucumber, diced
- 1 cup cherry tomatoes, halved
- 1/3 cup red onion, finely chopped
- 1/4 cup black olives, sliced
- 1/4 cup crumbled feta cheese
- 2 tablespoons fresh parsley, chopped
- Zest and juice of 1 lemon
- 3 tablespoons extra virgin olive oil
- 1 teaspoon dried oregano
- Salt and pepper to taste

Instructions:

1. In a large bowl, combine chickpeas, cucumber, cherry tomatoes, red onion, olives, feta cheese, and parsley.

2. In a small bowl, whisk together lemon zest, lemon juice, olive oil, dried oregano, salt, and pepper.

3. Pour the dressing over the salad and toss gently to coat.

4. Refrigerate for at least 30 minutes before serving.

5. Serve chilled, embracing the refreshing lemon and herb infusion.

Nutritional Values (per serving):

- Calories: 280 kcal
- Protein: 10g
- Carbohydrates: 29g
- Dietary Fiber: 8g
- Sugars: 5g
- Fat: 16g
- Saturated Fat: 3g
- Cholesterol: 10mg
- Sodium: 480mg

3. Avocado and Chickpea Mediterranean Salad:

Ingredients:

- 2 cans (15 oz each) chickpeas, drained and rinsed
- 1 avocado, diced
- 1 cup cherry tomatoes, halved
- 1/2 red onion, finely chopped
- 1/4 cup Kalamata olives, sliced
- 1/4 cup crumbled feta cheese
- 2 tablespoons fresh basil, chopped
- 3 tablespoons extra virgin olive oil
- 2 tablespoons balsamic vinegar
- Salt and pepper to taste

Instructions:

1. In a large bowl, combine chickpeas, avocado, cherry tomatoes, red onion, olives, feta cheese, and basil.

2. In a small bowl, whisk together olive oil, balsamic vinegar, salt, and pepper.

3. Pour the dressing over the salad and toss gently to combine.

4. Refrigerate for at least 30 minutes before serving.

5. Serve chilled, savoring the creamy texture of avocado.

Nutritional Values (per serving):

- Calories: 340 kcal
- Protein: 11g
- Carbohydrates: 30g
- Dietary Fiber: 9g
- Sugars: 5g
- Fat: 21g
- Saturated Fat: 4g
- Cholesterol: 10mg
- Sodium: 560mg

4. Quinoa Mediterranean Chickpea Salad:

Ingredients:

- 1 cup quinoa, cooked and cooled
- 2 cans (15 oz each) chickpeas, drained and rinsed
- 1 cucumber, diced
- 1 cup cherry tomatoes, halved
- 1/3 cup red onion, finely chopped
- 1/4 cup black olives, sliced
- 1/4 cup crumbled feta cheese
- 2 tablespoons fresh parsley, chopped
- 3 tablespoons extra virgin olive oil
- 2 tablespoons red wine vinegar
- 1 teaspoon dried oregano
- Salt and pepper to taste

Instructions:

1. In a large bowl, combine cooked quinoa, chickpeas, cucumber, cherry tomatoes, red onion, olives, feta cheese, and parsley.

2. In a small bowl, whisk together olive oil, red wine vinegar, dried oregano, salt, and pepper.

3. Pour the dressing over the salad and toss gently to combine.

4. Refrigerate for at least 30 minutes before serving.

5. Serve chilled, relishing the added protein and texture from quinoa.

Nutritional Values (per serving):

- Calories: 380 kcal
- Protein: 14g
- Carbohydrates: 46g
- Dietary Fiber: 10g
- Sugars: 5g
- Fat: 17g
- Saturated Fat: 3g
- Cholesterol: 10mg
- Sodium: 520mg

5. Spinach and Chickpea Mediterranean Salad:

Ingredients:

- 2 cans (15 oz each) chickpeas, drained and rinsed
- 3 cups fresh spinach leaves
- 1 cup cherry tomatoes, halved
- 1/3 cup red onion, finely chopped
- 1/4 cup crumbled feta cheese
- 1/4 cup pine nuts, toasted
- 3 tablespoons extra virgin olive oil
- 2 tablespoons balsamic vinegar
- 1 teaspoon honey
- Salt and pepper to taste

Instructions:

1. In a large bowl, combine chickpeas, fresh spinach, cherry tomatoes, red onion, feta cheese, and pine nuts.

2. In a small bowl, whisk together olive oil, balsamic vinegar, honey, salt, and pepper.

3. Pour the dressing over the salad and toss gently to coat.

4. Refrigerate for at least 30 minutes before serving.

5. Serve chilled, enjoying the vibrant flavors and nutritional benefits of fresh spinach.

Nutritional Values (per serving):

- Calories: 310 kcal
- Protein: 12g
- Carbohydrates: 30g
- Dietary Fiber: 8g
- Sugars: 5g
- Fat: 18g
- Saturated Fat: 3g
- Cholesterol: 10mg
- Sodium: 530mg

Why Mediterranean Chickpea Salad is nutrient-rich:

1. **Protein-Packed Chickpeas:**
    - Chickpeas are rich in plant-based protein, essential for muscle repair, immune function, and overall body maintenance.

2. **Abundance of Fiber:**
    - Incorporating vegetables and legumes ensures a high dietary fiber content, promoting digestive health, and contributing to a feeling of fullness.

3. **Healthy Fats from Olive Oil and Nuts:**
    - Extra virgin olive oil and nuts provide monounsaturated fats and omega-3 fatty acids, supporting heart health and providing a source of sustained energy.

4. **Antioxidant-Rich Ingredients:**

   - The variety of colorful vegetables and herbs contribute antioxidants, helping combat oxidative stress and inflammation in the body.

5. **Versatile Nutrient Profile:**

   - The combination of ingredients offers a well-rounded nutrient profile, including vitamins, minerals, and phytonutrients essential for overall well-being.

6. **Adaptable to Dietary Preferences:**

   - These recipes can be adapted to various dietary preferences, including vegetarian and gluten-free, ensuring accessibility to a wide range of individuals.

7. **Fresh and Wholesome Components:**

   - The use of fresh produce ensures a burst of flavors, while feta cheese adds a touch of creaminess, creating a salad that is both satisfying and delicious.

In summary, the Mediterranean Chickpea Salad is nutrient-rich due to its carefully chosen ingredients, offering a symphony of flavors and nutritional benefits. Each variation provides a unique experience while consistently delivering a wholesome and healthful meal option for those embracing a low-nickel lifestyle.

Avocado Bliss Wrap Recipes

Ingredients:

- 1 whole-grain wrap
- 1 ripe avocado, sliced
- 1 cup mixed greens (spinach, arugula, or kale)
- 1/2 cup cherry tomatoes, halved
- 1/4 cup red onion, thinly sliced
- 2 tablespoons hummus
- Salt and pepper to taste

Instructions:

1. Lay the whole-grain wrap flat on a clean surface.
2. Spread a layer of hummus over the wrap.
3. Arrange sliced avocado, mixed greens, cherry tomatoes, and red onion on the hummus.
4. Season with salt and pepper to taste.
5. Fold in the sides and roll the wrap tightly.
6. Slice in half diagonally and serve.

Nutritional Values (per serving):

- Calories: 350 kcal
- Protein: 8g
- Carbohydrates: 45g
- Dietary Fiber: 12g
- Sugars: 3g
- Fat: 18g

- Saturated Fat: 2g
- Cholesterol: 0mg
- Sodium: 450mg

2. Southwest Avocado Bliss Wrap:

Ingredients:

- 1 whole-grain wrap
- 1 ripe avocado, sliced
- 1/2 cup black beans, drained and rinsed
- 1/4 cup corn kernels (fresh or frozen, thawed)
- 1/4 cup red bell pepper, diced
- 2 tablespoons Greek yogurt or sour cream
- 1 tablespoon fresh cilantro, chopped
- Dash of cayenne pepper (optional)
- Salt and pepper to taste

Instructions:

1. Lay the whole-grain wrap flat on a clean surface.
2. Spread a layer of Greek yogurt or sour cream over the wrap.
3. Arrange sliced avocado, black beans, corn, and red bell pepper on the yogurt.
4. Sprinkle fresh cilantro and cayenne pepper if desired.
5. Season with salt and pepper to taste.
6. Fold in the sides and roll the wrap tightly.
7. Slice in half diagonally and serve.

Nutritional Values (per serving):

- Calories: 380 kcal
- Protein: 12g
- Carbohydrates: 50g
- Dietary Fiber: 14g
- Sugars: 4g
- Fat: 18g
- Saturated Fat: 3g
- Cholesterol: 5mg
- Sodium: 520mg

3. Grilled Chicken Avocado Bliss Wrap:

Ingredients:

- 1 whole-grain wrap
- 1 grilled chicken breast, sliced
- 1 ripe avocado, sliced
- 1 cup mixed greens (romaine, spinach, or arugula)
- 1/4 cup cherry tomatoes, halved
- 2 tablespoons Greek yogurt or tzatziki sauce
- 1 tablespoon fresh basil, chopped
- Salt and pepper to taste

Instructions:

1. Lay the whole-grain wrap flat on a clean surface.
2. Spread a layer of Greek yogurt or tzatziki sauce over the wrap.

3. Arrange sliced grilled chicken, avocado, mixed greens, and cherry tomatoes on the sauce.

4. Sprinkle fresh basil over the ingredients.

5. Season with salt and pepper to taste.

6. Fold in the sides and roll the wrap tightly.

7. Slice in half diagonally and serve.

Nutritional Values (per serving):

- Calories: 420 kcal
- Protein: 28g
- Carbohydrates: 35g
- Dietary Fiber: 10g
- Sugars: 4g
- Fat: 20g
- Saturated Fat: 3g
- Cholesterol: 65mg
- Sodium: 520mg

4. Quinoa Avocado Bliss Wrap:

Ingredients:

- 1 whole-grain wrap
- 1/½up cooked quinoa, cooled
- 1 ripe avocado, sliced
- 1/¼up cucumber, thinly sliced
- 1/¼up carrot, grated
- 2 tablespoons hummus
- 1 tablespoon fresh mint, chopped
- Lemon juice for drizzling
- Salt and pepper to taste

Instructions:

1. Lay the whole-grain wrap flat on a clean surface.
2. Spread a layer of hummus over the wrap.
3. Combine cooked quinoa, sliced avocado, cucumber, and grated carrot on the hummus.
4. Sprinkle fresh mint over the ingredients.
5. Drizzle with lemon juice and season with salt and pepper to taste.
6. Fold in the sides and roll the wrap tightly.
7. Slice in half diagonally and serve.

Nutritional Values (per serving):

- Calories: 340 kcal
- Protein: 8g
- Carbohydrates: 45g

- Dietary Fiber: 10g

- Sugars: 3g

- Fat: 16g

- Saturated Fat: 2g

- Cholesterol: 0mg

- Sodium: 450mg

Why Avocado Bliss Wrap is nutrient-rich:

1. **Heart-Healthy Fats:**

    - Avocado provides monounsaturated fats, promoting heart health and contributing to satiety.

2. **Fiber from Whole Grains and Vegetables:**

    - Whole-grain wraps and an abundance of vegetables offer dietary fiber, aiding digestion and supporting overall gut health.

3. **Protein-Packed Variations:**

    - The inclusion of proteins from sources like hummus, beans, chicken, quinoa, and tuna ensures a balanced and satisfying meal.

4. **Nutrient-Dense Ingredients:**

    - Fresh vegetables, herbs, and whole grains contribute essential vitamins, minerals, and antioxidants, promoting overall well-being.

5. **Customizable and Adaptable:**

    - These recipes are versatile and adaptable to various dietary preferences, ensuring accessibility to a wide range of individuals.

6. Balanced Macronutrient Profile:

- Each wrap offers a well-balanced profile of carbohydrates, proteins, and fats, supporting energy levels and metabolic functions.

In summary, the Avocado Bliss Wrap is a nutrient-rich and delicious meal option that combines the goodness of avocados with a variety of wholesome ingredients. These recipes cater to different taste preferences while consistently delivering a satisfying and healthful eating experience.

Thai Zoodle Bowl Extravaganza Recipes

1.Classic Thai Zoodle Bowl:

Ingredients:

- 2 medium zucchinis, spiralized
- 1 carrot, julienned
- 1/½up red bell pepper, thinly sliced
- 1/¼up shredded cabbage
- 1/¼up chopped scallions
- 1/¼up chopped peanuts
- 1/¼up fresh cilantro, chopped
- 1/¼up Thai basil leaves
- 1/3 cup tofu or grilled chicken, diced (optional)

Sauce:

- 3 tablespoons soy sauce (or tamari for gluten-free)
- 2 tablespoons lime juice
- 1 tablespoon sesame oil
- 1 tablespoon honey or agave
- 1 teaspoon ginger, grated
- 1 garlic clove, minced
- Red pepper flakes to taste

Instructions:

1. In a large bowl, combine zucchini noodles, julienned carrot, red bell pepper, shredded cabbage, scallions, peanuts, and tofu or grilled chicken if using.

2. In a separate bowl, whisk together soy sauce, lime juice, sesame oil, honey, ginger, garlic, and red pepper flakes to make the sauce.

3. Pour the sauce over the zoodle mixture and toss until well combined.

4. Garnish with fresh cilantro and Thai basil leaves.

5. Serve immediately and enjoy the classic Thai zoodle bowl.

Nutritional Values (per serving without tofu or chicken):

- Calories: 180 kcal
- Protein: 6g
- Carbohydrates: 22g
- Dietary Fiber: 5g
- Sugars: 11g
- Fat: 9g
- Saturated Fat: 1g
- Cholesterol: 0mg
- Sodium: 600mg

2. Spicy Peanut Thai Zoodle Bowl:

Ingredients:

- 2 medium zucchinis, spiralized
- 1 carrot, julienned
- 1/2 cup cucumber, thinly sliced
- 1/4 cup red onion, thinly sliced
- 1/4 cup edamame, shelled
- 2 tablespoons chopped peanuts
- 2 tablespoons fresh cilantro, chopped
- 1/3 cup cooked and shredded chicken or tofu

Sauce:

- 3 tablespoons peanut butter
- 2 tablespoons soy sauce (or tamari for gluten-free)
- 1 tablespoon rice vinegar
- 1 tablespoon lime juice
- 1 teaspoon Sriracha sauce (adjust to taste)
- 1 teaspoon honey or agave
- 1 garlic clove, minced

Instructions:

1. In a large bowl, combine zucchini noodles, julienned carrot, cucumber, red onion, edamame, chopped peanuts, and shredded chicken or tofu.

2. In a separate bowl, whisk together peanut butter, soy sauce, rice vinegar, lime juice, Sriracha, honey, and garlic to make the sauce.

3. Pour the sauce over the zoodle mixture and toss until well coated.

4. Garnish with fresh cilantro.

5. Serve immediately for a spicy peanut Thai zoodle bowl.

Nutritional Values (per serving with chicken or tofu):

- Calories: 250 kcal
- Protein: 15g
- Carbohydrates: 20g
- Dietary Fiber: 5g
- Sugars: 8g
- Fat: 14g
- Saturated Fat: 2g
- Cholesterol: 20mg
- Sodium: 700mg

3. Green Curry Thai Zoodle Bowl:

Ingredients:

- 2 medium zucchinis, spiralized
- 1 cup broccoli florets, steamed
- 1/2 cup snap peas, sliced
- 1/4 cup sliced bamboo shoots
- 1/4 cup sliced water chestnuts
- 1/4 cup chopped green onions
- 1/4 cup chopped cilantro
- 1/3 cup cooked shrimp or tofu

Sauce:

- 1/4 cup coconut milk
- 2 tablespoons green curry paste
- 1 tablespoon soy sauce (or tamari for gluten-free)
- 1 tablespoon lime juice
- 1 teaspoon fish sauce (omit for vegetarian/vegan)
- 1 teaspoon brown sugar

Instructions:

1. In a large bowl, combine zucchini noodles, steamed broccoli, snap peas, bamboo shoots, water chestnuts, green onions, cilantro, and shrimp or tofu.

2. In a small saucepan, whisk together coconut milk, green curry paste, soy sauce, lime juice, fish sauce, and brown sugar. Heat until well combined.

3. Pour the sauce over the zoodle mixture and toss until evenly coated.

4. Serve immediately for a flavorful green curry Thai zoodle bowl.

Nutritional Values (per serving with shrimp or tofu):

- Calories: 230 kcal
- Protein: 12g
- Carbohydrates: 20g
- Dietary Fiber: 5g
- Sugars: 6g
- Fat: 13g
- Saturated Fat: 7g
- Cholesterol: 50mg
- Sodium: 800mg

4. Mango Basil Thai Zoodle Bowl:

Ingredients:

- 2 medium zucchinis, spiralized
- 1 cup mango, julienned
- 1/2 cup red bell pepper, thinly sliced
- 1/4 cup red onion, thinly sliced
- 1/4 cup fresh basil leaves, torn
- 1/4 cup chopped cashews
- 1/3 cup grilled chicken or tofu

Sauce:

- 2 tablespoons soy sauce (or tamari for gluten-free)
- 1 tablespoon fish sauce (omit for vegetarian/vegan)
- 1 tablespoon lime juice

- 1 tablespoon honey or agave
- 1 teaspoon sesame oil
- 1/2 teaspoon ginger, grated

Instructions:

1. In a large bowl, combine zucchini noodles, julienned mango, red bell pepper, red onion, basil leaves, chopped cashews, and grilled chicken or tofu.

2. In a small bowl, whisk together soy sauce, fish sauce, lime juice, honey, sesame oil, and ginger to make the sauce.

3. Pour the sauce over the zoodle mixture and toss until well combined.

4. Serve immediately for a refreshing mango basil Thai zoodle bowl.

Nutritional Values (per serving with chicken or tofu):

- Calories: 260 kcal
- Protein: 13g
- Carbohydrates: 30g
- Dietary Fiber: 6g
- Sugars: 20g
- Fat: 12g
- Saturated Fat: 2g
- Cholesterol: 30mg
- Sodium: 700mg

5. Lemongrass Lime Thai Zoodle Bowl:

Ingredients:

- 2 medium zucchinis, spiralized
- 1 cup cherry tomatoes, halved
- 1/2 cup cucumber, thinly sliced
- 1/4 cup red onion, thinly sliced
- 1/4 cup fresh mint leaves, chopped
- 1/4 cup crushed peanuts
- 1/3 cup seared tofu or shrimp

Sauce:

- 2 tablespoons soy sauce (or tamari for gluten-free)
- 2 tablespoons lime juice
- 1 tablespoon lemongrass, minced
- 1 tablespoon fish sauce (omit for vegetarian/vegan)
- 1 tablespoon honey or agave
- 1 teaspoon sesame oil

Instructions:

1. In a large bowl, combine zucchini noodles, cherry tomatoes, cucumber, red onion, mint leaves, crushed peanuts, and seared tofu or shrimp.

2. In a small bowl, whisk together soy sauce, lime juice, lemongrass, fish sauce, honey, and sesame oil to make the sauce.

3. Pour the sauce over the zoodle mixture and toss until well coated.

4. Serve immediately for a zesty lemongrass lime Thai zoodle bowl.

Nutritional Values (per serving with tofu or shrimp):

- Calories: 240 kcal
- Protein: 10g
- Carbohydrates: 25g
- Dietary Fiber: 6g
- Sugars: 12g
- Fat: 13g
- Saturated Fat: 2g
- Cholesterol: 30mg
- Sodium: 600mg

Why Thai Zoodle Bowl Extravaganza is Nutrient-Rich:

1. **Abundance of Vegetables:**

   - Each recipe is loaded with a variety of colorful vegetables, providing essential vitamins, minerals, and antioxidants.

2. **Lean Protein Options:**

   - Whether it's tofu, grilled chicken, or shrimp, these recipes offer lean protein sources for muscle maintenance and overall satiety.

3. **Healthy Fats:**

   - Nuts and seeds used in the recipes contribute healthy fats, promoting heart health and aiding nutrient absorption.

4. **Low-Calorie, High-Nutrient Density:**

   - Zucchini noodles serve as a low-calorie base while offering fiber and nutrients, making the meals satisfying without excess calories.

5. **Customizable and Adaptable:**

- These recipes can be adapted to various dietary preferences, including vegetarian and vegan options, ensuring inclusivity.

6. **Vibrant Flavors:**

- The use of herbs, spices, and flavorful sauces enhances the taste, making these zoodle bowls a delicious and nutrient-rich choice.

In summary, the Thai Zoodle Bowl Extravaganza provides a burst of flavors, textures, and nutrients. Whether you prefer a classic version or a spicy peanut twist, these recipes offer a delightful and healthful alternative for those embracing a low-nickel lifestyle.

CHAPTER SIX
DINNER DELIGHTS

Culinary Magic for Evenings

As the sun sets and the day winds down, embark on a culinary journey that transforms your evenings into a delightful experience with the sub-chapter "Culinary Magic for Evenings." In this section of the "Low Nickel Diet Cookbook For Beginners," author Becky Mathew-Smith invites you to discover the enchantment of crafting nourishing and delectable dinners while adhering to a low-nickel lifestyle.

This segment of the cookbook serves as a gateway to a realm of flavors, carefully curated to bring joy and satisfaction to your evening meals. Becky Mathew-Smith, with her expertise in nutrition and allergy management, has designed a collection of dinner recipes that not only cater to the needs of those with nickel allergies but also elevate the dining experience for everyone at the table.

"Culinary Magic for Evenings" unveils a diverse array of recipes, ranging from comforting classics to innovative creations, all masterfully crafted to be low in nickel content without compromising on taste. Whether you're a seasoned chef or a beginner in the kitchen, this sub-chapter provides the guidance and inspiration needed to make each evening meal a culinary masterpiece.

From sumptuous one-pan wonders to aromatic and flavorful dishes, the recipes presented here showcase the versatility of a low-nickel diet. Imagine savoring dishes like Baked Salmon with Dill, Quinoa-Stuffed Bell Peppers, or Zoodle Alfredo—a testament to the creativity and ingenuity infused into every recipe.

Becky Mathew-Smith goes beyond merely offering recipes; she shares practical tips for meal preparation, ensuring that these evening delights seamlessly integrate into your daily routine. The focus is not just on restriction but on liberation—

liberation from dietary concerns and the assurance that your dinner plate can still be a canvas for culinary artistry.

As you delve into "Culinary Magic for Evenings," you'll find not only the satisfaction of a well-prepared meal but also the reassurance that your dietary choices contribute to your overall well-being. The recipes within this sub-chapter transcend the realm of restrictions, transforming dinner into a magical experience—one that delights the palate, nourishes the body, and brings joy to the soul.

Whether you're cooking for yourself, your family, or guests, the recipes in this section are crafted to impress. Each dish is a celebration of flavors, textures, and nutritional balance, embodying the essence of the entire cookbook—a guide that empowers you to reclaim your health and relish the joy of eating, even on a low-nickel diet.

So, let the enchantment of "Dinner Delights" captivate your evenings, making each meal a celebration of health, flavor, and the joy that comes from embracing a low-nickel lifestyle.

Citrus Glazed Salmon Recipes

1. **Classic Citrus Glazed Salmon:**

Ingredients:

- 4 salmon fillets (6 oz each)
- 1/4 cup orange juice
- 2 tablespoons lemon juice
- 2 tablespoons honey
- 1 tablespoon soy sauce (or tamari for gluten-free)
- 1 teaspoon grated ginger
- 2 cloves garlic, minced
- Salt and pepper to taste
- Sesame seeds and chopped green onions for garnish

Instructions:

1. Preheat the oven to 400°F (200°C).
2. In a bowl, whisk together orange juice, lemon juice, honey, soy sauce, grated ginger, and minced garlic to create the glaze.
3. Place salmon fillets on a baking sheet lined with parchment paper.
4. Brush the glaze generously over the salmon fillets.
5. Season with salt and pepper to taste.
6. Bake in the preheated oven for 12-15 minutes or until the salmon is cooked through.
7. Garnish with sesame seeds and chopped green onions.

8. Serve hot and enjoy the classic citrus glazed salmon.

Nutritional Values (per serving):

- Calories: 300 kcal
- Protein: 34g
- Carbohydrates: 12g
- Dietary Fiber: 0.5g
- Sugars: 10g
- Fat: 13g
- Saturated Fat: 2.5g
- Cholesterol: 90mg
- Sodium: 400mg

2. Zesty Lime Citrus Glazed Salmon:

Ingredients:

- 4 salmon fillets (6 oz each)
- 1/4 cup lime juice
- 2 tablespoons orange juice
- 2 tablespoons maple syrup
- 1 tablespoon Dijon mustard
- 1 teaspoon lime zest
- 2 cloves garlic, minced
- Salt and pepper to taste
- Fresh cilantro for garnish

Instructions:

1. Preheat the oven to 400°F (200°C).

2. In a bowl, whisk together lime juice, orange juice, maple syrup, Dijon mustard, lime zest, and minced garlic to create the glaze.

3. Place salmon fillets on a baking sheet lined with parchment paper.

4. Brush the glaze generously over the salmon fillets.

5. Season with salt and pepper to taste.

6. Bake in the preheated oven for 12-15 minutes or until the salmon is cooked through.

7. Garnish with fresh cilantro.

8. Serve hot and enjoy the zesty lime citrus glazed salmon.

Nutritional Values (per serving):

- Calories: 320 kcal
- Protein: 36g
- Carbohydrates: 14g
- Dietary Fiber: 0.5g
- Sugars: 10g
- Fat: 14g
- Saturated Fat: 2.5g
- Cholesterol: 95mg
- Sodium: 420mg

3. Honey Orange Citrus Glazed Salmon:

Ingredients:

- 4 salmon fillets (6 oz each)
- 1/4 cup orange juice
- 2 tablespoons honey
- 1 tablespoon rice vinegar
- 1 teaspoon soy sauce (or tamari for gluten-free)
- 1/2 teaspoon ground cumin
- 2 cloves garlic, minced
- Salt and pepper to taste
- Orange slices for garnish

Instructions:

1. Preheat the oven to 400°F (200°C).
2. In a bowl, whisk together orange juice, honey, rice vinegar, soy sauce, ground cumin, and minced garlic to create the glaze.
3. Place salmon fillets on a baking sheet lined with parchment paper.
4. Brush the glaze generously over the salmon fillets.
5. Season with salt and pepper to taste.
6. Bake in the preheated oven for 12-15 minutes or until the salmon is cooked through.
7. Garnish with orange slices.
8. Serve hot and enjoy the honey orange citrus glazed salmon.

Nutritional Values (per serving):

- Calories: 310 kcal
- Protein: 35g
- Carbohydrates: 15g
- Dietary Fiber: 0.5g
- Sugars: 12g
- Fat: 13g
- Saturated Fat: 2.5g
- Cholesterol: 90mg
- Sodium: 380mg

4. Grapefruit Ginger Citrus Glazed Salmon:

Ingredients:

- 4 salmon fillets (6 oz each)
- 1/4 cup grapefruit juice
- 2 tablespoons lemon juice
- 2 tablespoons honey
- 1 tablespoon fresh ginger, grated
- 1 teaspoon soy sauce (or tamari for gluten-free)
- 2 cloves garlic, minced
- Salt and pepper to taste
- Sliced green onions for garnish

Instructions:

1. Preheat the oven to 400°F (200°C).

2. In a bowl, whisk together grapefruit juice, lemon juice, honey, grated ginger, soy sauce, and minced garlic to create the glaze.

3. Place salmon fillets on a baking sheet lined with parchment paper.

4. Brush the glaze generously over the salmon fillets.

5. Season with salt and pepper to taste.

6. Bake in the preheated oven for 12-15 minutes or until the salmon is cooked through.

7. Garnish with sliced green onions.

8. Serve hot and enjoy the grapefruit ginger citrus glazed salmon.

Nutritional Values (per serving):

- Calories: 290 kcal
- Protein: 33g
- Carbohydrates: 13g
- Dietary Fiber: 0.5g
- Sugars: 11g
- Fat: 12g
- Saturated Fat: 2.5g
- Cholesterol: 85mg / Sodium: 390mg

5. Tangy Lemon Herb Citrus Glazed Salmon:

Ingredients:

- 4 salmon fillets (6 oz each)
- 1/4 cup lemon juice
- 2 tablespoons orange juice
- 2 tablespoons olive oil
- 1 tablespoon fresh parsley, chopped
- 1 teaspoon dried oregano
- 1 teaspoon Dijon mustard
- 2 cloves garlic, minced
- Salt and pepper to taste
- Lemon slices for garnish

Instructions:

1. Preheat the oven to 400°F (200°C).
2. In a bowl, whisk together lemon juice, orange juice, olive oil, chopped parsley, dried oregano, Dijon mustard, and minced garlic to create the glaze.
3. Place salmon fillets on a baking sheet lined with parchment paper.
4. Brush the glaze generously over the salmon fillets.
5. Season with salt and pepper to taste.
6. Bake in the preheated oven for 12-15 minutes or until the salmon is cooked through.
7. Garnish with lemon slices.

8. Serve hot and enjoy the tangy lemon herb citrus glazed salmon.

Nutritional Values (per serving):

- Calories: 330 kcal
- Protein: 37g
- Carbohydrates: 11g
- Dietary Fiber: 0.5g
- Sugars: 9g
- Fat: 16g
- Saturated Fat: 3g
- Cholesterol: 100mg
- Sodium: 410mg

Why Citrus Glazed Salmon is Nutrient-Rich:
1. **Rich in Omega-3 Fatty Acids:**

    - Salmon is a great source of omega-3 fatty acids, supporting heart health and reducing inflammation.

2. **Lean Protein:**

    - Salmon provides high-quality protein essential for muscle maintenance and overall body function.

3. **Vitamins and Minerals:**

    - Citrus fruits contribute vitamin C, while herbs and spices add essential minerals and antioxidants.

4. **Low-Calorie, High-Nutrient Density:**

- These recipes offer a balanced combination of macronutrients with relatively low calories, making them suitable for various dietary preferences.

5. **Versatile and Adaptable:**

- The variety of glazes allows for customization based on taste preferences, ensuring a delightful dining experience.

In summary, Citrus Glazed Salmon not only tantalizes the taste buds but also provides a nutrient-rich and healthful option for those following a low-nickel diet. Incorporate these recipes into your culinary repertoire for evenings filled with flavor, nutrition, and the satisfaction of a well-balanced meal.

Spiced Cauliflower Steaks Recipes

1. Classic Roasted Cauliflower Steaks:

Ingredients:

- 1 large cauliflower head, sliced into 1-inch steaks
- 2 tablespoons olive oil
- 1 teaspoon smoked paprika
- 1 teaspoon garlic powder
- 1/2 teaspoon cumin
- Salt and pepper to taste
- Fresh parsley for garnish

Instructions:

1. Preheat the oven to 425°F (220°C).
2. Place cauliflower steaks on a baking sheet lined with parchment paper.
3. In a bowl, mix olive oil, smoked paprika, garlic powder, cumin, salt, and pepper to create a spice rub.
4. Brush the spice rub over both sides of the cauliflower steaks.
5. Roast in the preheated oven for 25-30 minutes or until the cauliflower is tender and golden.
6. Garnish with fresh parsley.
7. Serve hot and enjoy the classic roasted cauliflower steaks.

Nutritional Values (per serving):

- Calories: 120 kcal

- Protein: 5g

- Carbohydrates: 12g

- Dietary Fiber: 5g

- Sugars: 4g

- Fat: 7g

- Saturated Fat: 1g

- Cholesterol: 0mg

- Sodium: 380mg

2. Turmeric and Ginger Cauliflower Steaks:

Ingredients:

- 1 large cauliflower head, sliced into 1-inch steaks

- 2 tablespoons olive oil

- 1 teaspoon ground turmeric

- 1 teaspoon ground ginger

- 1/2 teaspoon cayenne pepper

- Salt and pepper to taste

- Fresh cilantro for garnish

Instructions:

1. Preheat the oven to 425°F (220°C).

2. Place cauliflower steaks on a baking sheet lined with parchment paper.

3. In a bowl, mix olive oil, ground turmeric, ground ginger, cayenne pepper, salt, and pepper to create a spice blend.

4. Brush the spice blend over both sides of the cauliflower steaks.

5. Roast in the preheated oven for 25-30 minutes or until the cauliflower is tender and lightly browned.

6. Garnish with fresh cilantro.

7. Serve hot and enjoy the turmeric and ginger cauliflower steaks.

Nutritional Values (per serving):

- Calories: 130 kcal

- Protein: 5.5g

- Carbohydrates: 14g

- Dietary Fiber: 6g

- Sugars: 5g

- Fat: 7.5g

- Saturated Fat: 1g

- Cholesterol: 0mg

- Sodium: 390mg

3. Lemon Herb Cauliflower Steaks:

Ingredients:

- 1 large cauliflower head, sliced into 1-inch steaks

- 2 tablespoons olive oil

- Zest and juice of 1 lemon

- 1 teaspoon dried thyme

- 1 teaspoon dried rosemary

- Salt and pepper to taste

- Fresh chives for garnish

Instructions:

1. Preheat the oven to 425°F (220°C).

2. Place cauliflower steaks on a baking sheet lined with parchment paper.

3. In a bowl, mix olive oil, lemon zest, lemon juice, dried thyme, dried rosemary, salt, and pepper to create a herb-infused marinade.

4. Brush the marinade over both sides of the cauliflower steaks.

5. Roast in the preheated oven for 25-30 minutes or until the cauliflower is tender and aromatic.

6. Garnish with fresh chives.

7. Serve hot and enjoy the lemon herb cauliflower steaks.

Nutritional Values (per serving):

- Calories: 140 kcal
- Protein: 6g
- Carbohydrates: 15g
- Dietary Fiber: 6.5g
- Sugars: 5.5g
- Fat: 7.5g
- Saturated Fat: 1g
- Cholesterol: 0mg
- Sodium: 400mg

4. Balsamic Glazed Cauliflower Steaks:

Ingredients:

- 1 large cauliflower head, sliced into 1-inch steaks
- 2 tablespoons olive oil
- 3 tablespoons balsamic vinegar
- 1 tablespoon Dijon mustard
- 1 teaspoon honey or maple syrup
- Salt and pepper to taste
- Fresh basil for garnish

Instructions:

1. Preheat the oven to 425°F (220°C).
2. Place cauliflower steaks on a baking sheet lined with parchment paper.
3. In a bowl, whisk together olive oil, balsamic vinegar, Dijon mustard, honey or maple syrup, salt, and pepper to create a balsamic glaze.
4. Brush the balsamic glaze over both sides of the cauliflower steaks.
5. Roast in the preheated oven for 25-30 minutes or until the cauliflower is tender and glazed.
6. Garnish with fresh basil.
7. Serve hot and enjoy the balsamic glazed cauliflower steaks.

Nutritional Values (per serving):

- Calories: 150 kcal
- Protein: 6.5g

- Carbohydrates: 16g

- Dietary Fiber: 6.5g

- Sugars: 7g

- Fat: 8g

- Saturated Fat: 1g

- Cholesterol: 0mg

- Sodium: 410mg

5. Curry Spiced Cauliflower Steaks:

Ingredients:

- 1 large cauliflower head, sliced into 1-inch steaks

- 2 tablespoons olive oil

- 1 tablespoon curry powder

- 1 teaspoon ground cumin

- 1 teaspoon ground coriander

- Salt and pepper to taste

- Fresh mint for garnish

Instructions:

1. Preheat the oven to 425°F (220°C).

2. Place cauliflower steaks on a baking sheet lined with parchment paper.

3. In a bowl, mix olive oil, curry powder, ground cumin, ground coriander, salt, and pepper to create a curry spice blend.

4. Brush the spice blend over both sides of the cauliflower steaks.

5. Roast in the preheated oven for 25-30 minutes or until the cauliflower is tender and aromatic.

6. Garnish with fresh mint.

7. Serve hot and enjoy the curry spiced cauliflower steaks.

Nutritional Values (per serving):

- Calories: 140 kcal
- Protein: 5.5g
- Carbohydrates: 14g
- Dietary Fiber: 5.5g
- Sugars: 4.5g
- Fat: 7.5g
- Saturated Fat: 1g
- Cholesterol: 0mg
- Sodium: 380mg

Why Spiced Cauliflower Steaks are Nutrient-Rich:
1. **Rich in Fiber:**

    - Cauliflower is a good source of dietary fiber, promoting digestive health and providing a sense of fullness.

2. **Low-Calorie Option:**

    - These recipes offer a nutrient-dense, low-calorie alternative for those seeking flavorful yet healthful meals.

3. **Antioxidant-Rich Spices:**

- The inclusion of various spices adds not only flavor but also antioxidants, supporting overall well-being.

4. **Versatile and Adaptable:**

- Spice blends can be customized to personal taste preferences, ensuring a diverse and enjoyable culinary experience.

5. **Gluten-Free and Plant-Based:**

- These recipes are suitable for individuals following gluten-free and plant-based diets, enhancing inclusivity.

In summary, Spiced Cauliflower Steaks provide a delicious and nutrient-rich option for those embracing a low-nickel lifestyle. Incorporate these recipes into your meal rotation for a flavorful and healthful dining experience.

Harvest Stuffed Bell Peppers Recipes

1. Quinoa and black bean harvest stuffed peppers:

Ingredients:

- 4 large bell peppers, halved
- 1 cup cooked quinoa
- 1 cup black beans, cooked
- 1 cup corn kernels (fresh or frozen)
- 1 cup cherry tomatoes, diced
- 1/2 cup red onion, finely chopped
- 1/2 cup cilantro, chopped
- 1 teaspoon cumin
- 1 teaspoon smoked paprika
- Salt and pepper to taste
- 1 cup shredded cheddar cheese (optional)

Instructions:

1. Preheat the oven to 375°F (190°C).
2. In a bowl, combine cooked quinoa, black beans, corn, cherry tomatoes, red onion, cilantro, cumin, smoked paprika, salt, and pepper.
3. Fill each bell pepper half with the quinoa and black bean mixture.
4. If desired, top each stuffed pepper with shredded cheddar cheese.
5. Place the stuffed peppers in a baking dish.
6. Bake in the preheated oven for 25-30 minutes or until the peppers are tender.

7. Remove from the oven and let them cool slightly before serving.

8. Enjoy the Quinoa and Black Bean Harvest Stuffed Peppers.

Nutritional Values (per serving):

- Calories: 280 kcal

- Protein: 11g

- Carbohydrates: 48g

- Dietary Fiber: 10g

- Sugars: 5g

- Fat: 5g

- Saturated Fat: 2g

- Cholesterol: 10mg

- Sodium: 220mg

Nutrient-Rich Explanation:

- **Quinoa and Black Beans:** Rich in protein and essential nutrients, these ingredients provide a balanced and plant-based protein source suitable for a low-nickel diet.

- **Bell Peppers:** Packed with vitamin C and antioxidants, bell peppers contribute to overall immune health and well-being.

- **Corn and Cherry Tomatoes:** Adding natural sweetness and fiber, corn and cherry tomatoes enhance the taste while providing essential nutrients.

- **Cilantro:** Apart from its aromatic flavor, cilantro contributes vitamins and minerals, promoting overall health.

- **Cheese (Optional):** For those not sensitive to nickel, the optional cheese adds calcium and protein, enhancing the nutritional profile.

2. Lentil and Vegetable Harvest Stuffed Peppers:

Ingredients:

- 4 large bell peppers, halved
- 1 cup cooked lentils
- 1 cup zucchini, diced
- 1 cup carrots, grated
- 1 cup spinach, chopped
- 1/2 cup red onion, finely chopped
- 2 cloves garlic, minced
- 1 teaspoon Italian seasoning
- Salt and pepper to taste
- 1 cup feta cheese, crumbled (optional)

Instructions:

1. Preheat the oven to 375°F (190°C).
2. In a bowl, combine cooked lentils, zucchini, carrots, spinach, red onion, garlic, Italian seasoning, salt, and pepper.
3. Fill each bell pepper half with the lentil and vegetable mixture.

4. If desired, top each stuffed pepper with crumbled feta cheese.

5. Place the stuffed peppers in a baking dish.

6. Bake in the preheated oven for 25-30 minutes or until the peppers are tender.

7. Remove from the oven and let them cool slightly before serving.

8. Enjoy the Lentil and Vegetable Harvest Stuffed Peppers.

Nutritional Values (per serving):

- Calories: 260 kcal

- Protein: 14g

- Carbohydrates: 40g

- Dietary Fiber: 11g

- Sugars: 7g

- Fat: 6g

- Saturated Fat: 3g

- Cholesterol: 15mg

- Sodium: 280mg

Nutrient-Rich Explanation:

- **Lentils:** Packed with protein and fiber, lentils contribute to satiety and provide essential nutrients for overall health.

- **Zucchini, Carrots, and Spinach:** These vegetables offer a spectrum of vitamins, minerals, and antioxidants, supporting a well-rounded diet.

- **Feta Cheese (Optional):** For those not sensitive to nickel, feta cheese adds a creamy texture along with calcium and protein.

3. Turkey and Quinoa Harvest Stuffed Peppers:

Ingredients:

- 4 large bell peppers, halved
- 1 cup cooked quinoa
- 1 lb ground turkey
- 1 cup butternut squash, diced
- 1/2 cup red onion, finely chopped
- 1/2 cup cranberries, dried
- 1 teaspoon ground sage
- Salt and pepper to taste
- 1/2 cup feta cheese, crumbled (optional)

Instructions:

1. Preheat the oven to 375°F (190°C).
2. In a skillet, cook ground turkey until browned. Add diced butternut squash and cook until tender.
3. In a bowl, combine cooked quinoa, turkey and butternut squash mixture, red onion, dried cranberries, ground sage, salt, and pepper.
4. Fill each bell pepper half with the turkey and quinoa mixture.
5. If desired, top each stuffed pepper with crumbled feta cheese.
6. Place the stuffed peppers in a baking dish.

7. Bake in the preheated oven for 25-30 minutes or until the peppers are tender.

8. Remove from the oven and let them cool slightly before serving.

9. Enjoy the Turkey and Quinoa Harvest Stuffed Peppers.

Nutritional Values (per serving):

- Calories: 330 kcal

- Protein: 22g

- Carbohydrates: 43g

- Dietary Fiber: 7g

- Sugars: 11g

- Fat: 9g

- Saturated Fat: 3g

- Cholesterol: 55mg

- Sodium: 320mg

Nutrient-Rich Explanation:

- **Turkey:** A lean protein source providing essential amino acids for muscle maintenance.

- **Butternut Squash:** Rich in vitamins and antioxidants, contributing to overall well-being.

- **Cranberries:** Adding natural sweetness, cranberries provide antioxidants and support urinary tract health.

- **Feta Cheese (Optional):** For those not sensitive to nickel, feta cheese complements the dish with additional protein and calcium.

4. Chickpea and Mediterranean Harvest Stuffed Peppers:

Ingredients:

- 4 large bell peppers, halved
- 1 cup cooked quinoa
- 1 can chickpeas, drained and rinsed
- 1 cup cucumber, diced
- 1 cup cherry tomatoes, halved
- 1/2 cup red onion, finely chopped
- 1/4 cup Kalamata olives, sliced
- 1/4 cup feta cheese, crumbled
- 2 tablespoons olive oil
- 1 teaspoon dried oregano
- Salt and pepper to taste

Instructions:

1. Preheat the oven to 375°F (190°C).
2. In a bowl, combine cooked quinoa, chickpeas, cucumber, cherry tomatoes, red onion, Kalamata olives, feta cheese, olive oil, dried oregano, salt, and pepper.
3. Fill each bell pepper half with the chickpea and Mediterranean mixture.
4. Place the stuffed peppers in a baking dish.
5. Bake in the preheated oven for 25-30 minutes or until the peppers are tender.
6. Remove from the oven and let them cool slightly before serving.

7. Enjoy the Chickpea and Mediterranean Harvest Stuffed Peppers.

Nutritional Values (per serving):

- Calories: 290 kcal

- Protein: 11g

- Carbohydrates: 40g

- Dietary Fiber: 9g

- Sugars: 8g

- Fat: 11g

- Saturated Fat: 3g

- Cholesterol: 10mg

- Sodium: 380mg

Nutrient-Rich Explanation:

- **Chickpeas:** A plant-based protein source with fiber, promoting digestive health and satiety.

- **Mediterranean Ingredients:** Cucumber, tomatoes, olives, and olive oil provide a range of vitamins, minerals, and heart-healthy fats.

- **Feta Cheese:** For those not sensitive to nickel, feta cheese adds a creamy texture along with calcium and protein.

5. Tofu and Vegetable Harvest Stuffed Peppers:

Ingredients:

- 4 large bell peppers, halved
- 1 cup cooked brown rice
- 1 cup firm tofu, diced
- 1 cup broccoli florets, chopped
- 1 cup bell peppers (any color), diced
- 1/2 cup snow peas, sliced
- 1/2 cup carrot, shredded
- 2 tablespoons soy sauce
- 1 tablespoon sesame oil
- 1 teaspoon ginger, minced
- 1 teaspoon garlic, minced
- Sesame seeds for garnish

Instructions:

1. Preheat the oven to 375°F (190°C).
2. In a bowl, combine cooked brown rice, diced tofu, broccoli, bell peppers, snow peas, carrot, soy sauce, sesame oil, minced ginger, and minced garlic.
3. Fill each bell pepper half with the tofu and vegetable mixture.
4. Place the stuffed peppers in a baking dish.
5. Bake in the preheated oven for 25-30 minutes or until the peppers are tender.

6. Remove from the oven and let them cool slightly before serving.

7. Garnish with sesame seeds.

8. Enjoy the Tofu and Vegetable Harvest Stuffed Peppers.

Nutritional Values (per serving):

- Calories: 280 kcal

- Protein: 15g

- Carbohydrates: 41g

- Dietary Fiber: 7g

- Sugars: 5g

- Fat: 8g

- Saturated Fat: 1.5g

- Cholesterol: 0mg

- Sodium: 470mg

Nutrient-Rich Explanation:

- **Tofu:** A plant-based protein source that adds texture and substance to the dish.

- **Brown Rice:** A whole grain providing complex carbohydrates and dietary fiber for sustained energy.

- **Colorful Vegetables:** Broccoli, bell peppers, snow peas, and carrots offer a variety of vitamins, minerals, and antioxidants.

- **Soy Sauce and Sesame Oil:** Enhance flavor while providing a savory umami element.

Why Harvest Stuffed Bell Peppers are Nutrient-Rich for a Low Nickel Diet:

1. **Plant-Based Protein Sources:**

   - Incorporating beans, lentils, chickpeas, and tofu provides protein without the nickel content found in some animal products.

2. **Abundance of Vegetables:**

   - Bell peppers, tomatoes, zucchini, spinach, and other vegetables contribute essential nutrients without the worry of high nickel content.

3. **Whole Grains for Satiety:**

   - Quinoa, brown rice, and other whole grains offer dietary fiber and sustained energy, enhancing the nutritional profile of each recipe.

4. **Low-Nickel Optional Ingredients:**

   - Feta cheese is included as an optional topping, allowing those less sensitive to nickel to enjoy added flavor and nutrition.

5. **Balanced Macronutrients:**

   - Each recipe is carefully crafted to provide a balanced mix of protein, carbohydrates, and healthy fats, ensuring a satisfying and well-rounded meal.

Harvest Stuffed Bell Peppers offer a delightful array of flavors and textures while prioritizing nutrient-rich ingredients suitable for those following a low-nickel diet. These recipes provide a versatile and delicious option for individuals seeking a wholesome and flavorful dining experience.

CHAPTER SEVEN
SAVORY SOUPS FOR THE SOUL

Nourishing Elixirs

In the culinary journey through the "Low Nickel Diet Cookbook For Beginners," Chapter 7 emerges as a comforting oasis with its sub-chapter, 'Nourishing Elixirs.' As we delve into the heart of this chapter, readers are treated to a collection of soul-warming soups designed to nourish both the body and the spirit. The focus here is not just on flavors and textures but on crafting elixirs that soothe, replenish, and align with the principles of a low-nickel lifestyle.

Exploring the Essence: The 'Nourishing Elixirs' sub-chapter begins by inviting readers to savor the essence of homemade soups—each bowl a potion carefully concocted to provide not just sustenance but a profound sense of well-being. The emphasis is on creating elixirs that resonate with the nurturing spirit of home-cooked meals, bridging the gap between health-conscious choices and the undeniable joy of sipping on a comforting broth.

Tailored for Wellness: Every recipe within this sub-chapter is thoughtfully crafted to align with the dietary principles of a low-nickel lifestyle. Ingredients are selected not only for their delicious flavors but also for their nutritional value and compatibility with nickel restrictions. Readers can expect a diverse array of soups that feature fresh vegetables, lean proteins, and wholesome grains—each element chosen to provide warmth and nourishment without compromising on taste.

A Symphony of Flavors: From classic favorites like Minestrone to inventive blends like Coconut Curry Lentil Soup, 'Nourishing Elixirs' transforms the ordinary act of soup-making into a culinary symphony. Each recipe is a melody of flavors, striking a harmonious balance between health-conscious choices and the pleasure derived from a well-crafted bowl of soup. The chapter encourages experimentation with herbs, spices, and unique combinations, offering a delightful journey for the taste buds.

A Culinary Hug: In the realm of 'Nourishing Elixirs,' soup becomes more than just a meal—it becomes a culinary hug, wrapping readers in warmth and care. The carefully curated recipes extend beyond nourishing the body; they speak to the soul, evoking a sense of comfort reminiscent of home-cooked goodness. This sub-chapter is an invitation to slow down, savor each spoonful, and find solace in the art of crafting healing elixirs.

Practical Wellness: Building on the foundation laid in earlier chapters, 'Nourishing Elixirs' equips readers with practical tools for maintaining a low-nickel lifestyle. It provides insights into ingredient selection, portion control, and mindful eating, ensuring that every spoonful contributes not only to the joy of dining but also to the holistic well-being of the individual.

'Savory Soups for the Soul'—specifically the sub-chapter 'Nourishing Elixirs'—is a testament to the transformative power of thoughtful, health-conscious cooking. It is an ode to the simple yet profound pleasure of enjoying a bowl of soup that not only tantalizes the taste buds but also nourishes the body and soul. As readers embark on this culinary journey, they are encouraged to embrace the therapeutic essence of each elixir, savoring the richness of flavors and the comfort of a well-loved dish.

Minestrone Wellness Soup

Ingredients:

- 1 cup carrots, diced
- 1 cup celery, chopped
- 1 cup zucchini, diced
- 1 cup green beans, cut into small pieces
- 1 can (14 oz) diced tomatoes, undrained
- 1/2 cup quinoa, uncooked
- 4 cups vegetable broth (low-nickel)
- 1 teaspoon dried oregano
- 1 teaspoon dried basil
- Salt and pepper to taste
- 1/4 cup fresh parsley, chopped

Instructions:

1. In a large pot, combine carrots, celery, zucchini, green beans, diced tomatoes, quinoa, vegetable broth, oregano, basil, salt, and pepper.

2. Bring the mixture to a boil, then reduce heat and simmer for 20-25 minutes or until vegetables and quinoa are tender.

3. Adjust seasoning if needed.

4. Stir in fresh parsley before serving.

5. Enjoy the Minestrone Wellness Soup.

Nutritional Values (per serving):

- Calories: 180 kcal

- Protein: 5g

- Carbohydrates: 35g

- Dietary Fiber: 6g

- Sugars: 7g

- Fat: 1g

- Saturated Fat: 0g

- Cholesterol: 0mg

- Sodium: 550mg

Why it's Nutrient-Rich for a Low-Nickel Lifestyle:

- **Quinoa:** A low-nickel grain providing protein, fiber, and essential amino acids.

- **Vegetables:** Carrots, celery, zucchini, and green beans offer vitamins, minerals, and antioxidants without high nickel content.

- **Herbs:** Oregano and basil enhance flavor without contributing to nickel sensitivity.

- **Low-Nickel Broth:** Using vegetable broth specifically chosen for its low-nickel content ensures a safe and flavorful base.

2. Coconut Curry Lentil Soothe

Ingredients:

- 1 cup red lentils, rinsed
- 1 can (14 oz) coconut milk
- 1 cup sweet potatoes, diced
- 1 cup spinach, chopped
- 1 tablespoon red curry paste
- 1 teaspoon turmeric
- 1 teaspoon cumin
- Salt to taste
- Fresh cilantro for garnish

Instructions:

1. In a pot, combine red lentils, coconut milk, sweet potatoes, spinach, red curry paste, turmeric, cumin, and salt.
2. Bring to a simmer and cook for 20-25 minutes or until lentils and sweet potatoes are tender.
3. Adjust seasoning if needed.
4. Garnish with fresh cilantro before serving.
5. Enjoy the Coconut Curry Lentil Soothe.

Nutritional Values (per serving):

- Calories: 240 kcal
- Protein: 12g
- Carbohydrates: 30g
- Dietary Fiber: 8g

- Sugars: 3g

- Fat: 8g

- Saturated Fat: 6g

- Cholesterol: 0mg

- Sodium: 300mg

Why it's Nutrient-Rich for a Low-Nickel Lifestyle:

- **Red Lentils:** A protein and fiber source without high nickel content.

- **Coconut Milk:** Provides a creamy texture without nickel concerns.

- **Sweet Potatoes and Spinach:** Nutrient-dense vegetables offering vitamins and minerals.

- **Herbs and Spices:** Turmeric, cumin, and fresh cilantro add flavor without nickel-related issues.

3. Tomato Basil Harmony Broth

Ingredients:

- 4 cups low-nickel vegetable broth

- 1 can (28 oz) crushed tomatoes

- 1 cup carrots, shredded

- 1 cup celery, thinly sliced

- 1/2 cup fresh basil, chopped

- 2 cloves garlic, minced

- Salt and pepper to taste

- 1 tablespoon olive oil

Instructions:

1. In a pot, heat olive oil and sauté garlic until fragrant.

2. Add low-nickel vegetable broth, crushed tomatoes, shredded carrots, sliced celery, basil, salt, and pepper.

3. Simmer for 15-20 minutes.

4. Adjust seasoning if needed.

5. Serve hot and enjoy the Tomato Basil Harmony Broth.

Nutritional Values (per serving):

- Calories: 120 kcal
- Protein: 3g
- Carbohydrates: 20g
- Dietary Fiber: 4g
- Sugars: 8g
- Fat: 4g
- Saturated Fat: 0.5g
- Cholesterol: 0mg
- Sodium: 650mg

Why it's Nutrient-Rich for a Low-Nickel Lifestyle:

- **Vegetable Broth:** Specifically chosen for its low-nickel content, providing a safe base.

- **Crushed Tomatoes:** A rich source of antioxidants without high nickel levels.

- **Fresh Basil:** Adds flavor without contributing to nickel sensitivity.

- **Olive Oil:** Enhances richness and healthy fats without nickel concerns.

4. Ginger Turmeric Healing Broth

Ingredients:

- 4 cups low-nickel vegetable broth
- 1 tablespoon fresh ginger, grated
- 1 teaspoon ground turmeric
- 1 cup bok choy, chopped
- 1 cup shiitake mushrooms, sliced
- 1 cup rice noodles, cooked
- 2 green onions, sliced
- Soy sauce to taste

Instructions:

1. In a pot, combine low-nickel vegetable broth, grated ginger, ground turmeric, bok choy, and shiitake mushrooms.
2. Simmer for 15-20 minutes.
3. Add cooked rice noodles and soy sauce to taste.
4. Stir well and heat through.
5. Serve hot, garnished with sliced green onions.
6. Enjoy the Ginger Turmeric Healing Broth.

Nutritional Values (per serving):

- Calories: 180 kcal
- Protein: 6g
- Carbohydrates: 38g
- Dietary Fiber: 3g

- Sugars: 2g

- Fat: 1g

- Saturated Fat: 0g

- Cholesterol: 0mg

- Sodium: 600mg

Why it's Nutrient-Rich for a Low-Nickel Lifestyle:

- **Ginger and Turmeric:** Anti-inflammatory ingredients that add flavor without nickel concerns.

- **Bok Choy and Shiitake Mushrooms:** Nutrient-dense vegetables chosen for their low-nickel content.

- **Rice Noodles:** A gluten-free and low-nickel alternative for a comforting texture.

5. Butternut Squash Serenity Soup

Ingredients:

- 1 butternut squash, peeled and diced

- 1 onion, chopped

- 2 apples, peeled and diced

- 4 cups low-nickel vegetable broth

- 1 teaspoon ground cinnamon

- 1/2 teaspoon nutmeg

- Salt and pepper to taste

- 1/4 cup coconut milk (optional)

Instructions:

1. In a pot, combine butternut squash, chopped onion, diced apples, low-nickel vegetable broth, ground cinnamon, nutmeg, salt, and pepper.

2. Bring to a boil, then reduce heat and simmer for 20-25 minutes or until vegetables are tender.

3. Use an immersion blender to puree the soup until smooth.

4. If desired, stir in coconut milk for added creaminess.

5. Adjust seasoning if needed.

6. Serve hot and enjoy the Butternut Squash Serenity Soup.

Nutritional Values (per serving):

- Calories: 160 kcal

- Protein: 2g

- Carbohydrates: 40g

- Dietary Fiber: 7g

- Sugars: 12g

- Fat: 1g

- Saturated Fat: 0.5g

- Cholesterol: 0mg

- Sodium: 480mg

Why it's Nutrient-Rich for a Low-Nickel Lifestyle:

- **Butternut Squash and Apples:** Provide natural sweetness and essential nutrients without high nickel content.

- **Coconut Milk (Optional):** For those less sensitive to nickel, it adds creaminess and healthy fats.

- **Ground Cinnamon and Nutmeg:** Flavor enhancers without contributing to nickel-related concerns.

These 'Nourishing Elixirs' recipes are meticulously designed to align with the principles of a low-nickel lifestyle. They showcase a harmonious blend of ingredients that not only soothe the soul but also prioritize the well-being of individuals managing nickel sensitivities. Each bowl is a testament to the idea that wholesome, nutrient-rich soups can be both delicious and compatible with dietary restrictions, offering a comforting culinary experience for everyone on a low-nickel journey.

Roasted Tomato Basil Soup

1. Classic Roasted Tomato Basil Soup

Ingredients:

- 8 cups tomatoes, halved
- 1 large onion, quartered
- 6 cloves garlic, peeled
- 2 tablespoons olive oil
- Salt and pepper to taste
- 4 cups low-nickel vegetable broth
- 1 cup fresh basil leaves, packed
- 1 teaspoon dried oregano
- 1/2 teaspoon red pepper flakes (optional)
- 1/4 cup balsamic vinegar
- Fresh basil leaves for garnish

Instructions:

1. Preheat the oven to 400°F (200°C).
2. Place halved tomatoes, quartered onion, and peeled garlic cloves on a baking sheet.
3. Drizzle with olive oil and season with salt and pepper. Toss to coat evenly.
4. Roast in the oven for 30-40 minutes or until the tomatoes are caramelized.
5. In a large pot, combine the roasted vegetables, low-nickel vegetable broth, fresh basil, dried oregano, and red pepper flakes if using.

6. Bring to a simmer and cook for an additional 15-20 minutes to meld flavors.

7. Use an immersion blender to puree the soup until smooth.

8. Stir in balsamic vinegar.

9. Adjust seasoning if needed.

10. Serve hot, garnished with fresh basil leaves.

Nutritional Values (per serving):

- Calories: 180 kcal
- Protein: 5g
- Carbohydrates: 25g
- Dietary Fiber: 6g
- Sugars: 12g
- Fat: 8g
- Saturated Fat: 1.5g
- Cholesterol: 0mg
- Sodium: 650mg

Why it's Nutrient-Rich for a Low-Nickel Lifestyle:

- **Tomatoes:** A low-nickel fruit high in vitamins A and C.
- **Onion and Garlic:** Flavorful additions without significant nickel content.
- **Basil:** Adds freshness and antioxidants without contributing to nickel sensitivity.
- **Vegetable Broth:** Specifically chosen for its low-nickel content, providing a safe base.

- **Balsamic Vinegar:** Enhances flavor without high nickel levels.

2. Creamy Tomato Basil Coconut Soup

Ingredients:

- 8 cups tomatoes, halved
- 1 large onion, quartered
- 6 cloves garlic, peeled
- 2 tablespoons olive oil
- Salt and pepper to taste
- 4 cups low-nickel vegetable broth
- 1 cup fresh basil leaves, packed
- 1 teaspoon dried oregano
- 1 can (14 oz) coconut milk
- Fresh basil leaves and coconut cream for garnish

Instructions:

1. Follow steps 1-6 from the Classic Roasted Tomato Basil Soup recipe.
2. Add coconut milk to the pot and stir until well combined.
3. Continue to simmer for an additional 5-10 minutes.
4. Use an immersion blender to puree the soup until smooth.
5. Adjust seasoning if needed.
6. Serve hot, garnished with fresh basil leaves and a drizzle of coconut cream.

Nutritional Values (per serving):

- Calories: 220 kcal

- Protein: 5g

- Carbohydrates: 28g

- Dietary Fiber: 7g

- Sugars: 14g

- Fat: 12g

- Saturated Fat: 8g

- Cholesterol: 0mg

- Sodium: 670mg

Why it's Nutrient-Rich for a Low-Nickel Lifestyle:

- **Tomatoes, Onion, Garlic, Basil:** As in the Classic Roasted Tomato Basil Soup.

- **Coconut Milk:** Adds creaminess and healthy fats for those less sensitive to nickel.

3. Roasted Red Pepper Tomato Basil Soup

Ingredients:

- 8 cups tomatoes, halved

- 2 large red bell peppers, halved and seeds removed

- 1 large onion, quartered

- 6 cloves garlic, peeled

- 2 tablespoons olive oil

- Salt and pepper to taste

- 4 cups low-nickel vegetable broth

- 1 cup fresh basil leaves, packed
- 1 teaspoon dried oregano
- Fresh basil leaves for garnish

Instructions:

1. Preheat the oven to 400°F (200°C).
2. Place halved tomatoes, red bell peppers, quartered onion, and peeled garlic cloves on a baking sheet.
3. Drizzle with olive oil and season with salt and pepper. Toss to coat evenly.
4. Roast in the oven for 30-40 minutes or until the tomatoes are caramelized.
5. In a large pot, combine the roasted vegetables, low-nickel vegetable broth, fresh basil, and dried oregano.
6. Bring to a simmer and cook for an additional 15-20 minutes to meld flavors.
7. Use an immersion blender to puree the soup until smooth.
8. Adjust seasoning if needed.
9. Serve hot, garnished with fresh basil leaves.

Nutritional Values (per serving):

- Calories: 160 kcal
- Protein: 4g
- Carbohydrates: 28g
- Dietary Fiber: 7g
- Sugars: 15g

- Fat: 5g

- Saturated Fat: 0.5g

- Cholesterol: 0mg

- Sodium: 610mg

Why it's Nutrient-Rich for a Low-Nickel Lifestyle:

- **Tomatoes, Onion, Garlic, Basil:** As in the Classic Roasted Tomato Basil Soup.

- **Red Bell Peppers:** A low-nickel vegetable rich in vitamin C.

- **Vegetable Broth:** Specifically chosen for its low-nickel content, providing a safe base.

4. Rustic Tomato Basil Lentil Soup

Ingredients:

- 1 cup brown lentils, rinsed

- 6 cups low-nickel vegetable broth

- 8 cups tomatoes, diced

- 1 large onion, diced

- 4 cloves garlic, minced

- 2 tablespoons olive oil

- Salt and pepper to taste

- 1 cup fresh basil leaves, chopped

- 1 teaspoon dried thyme

- Fresh basil leaves for garnish

Instructions:

1. In a pot, combine brown lentils and low-nickel vegetable broth. Bring to a boil, then reduce heat and simmer for 25-30 minutes or until lentils are tender.

2. In a separate pan, sauté diced onion and minced garlic in olive oil until softened.

3. Add diced tomatoes to the pan and cook until they release their juices.

4. Combine the lentil mixture with the sautéed vegetables.

5. Season with salt, pepper, fresh basil, and dried thyme.

6. Simmer for an additional 10-15 minutes.

7. Adjust seasoning if needed.

8. Serve hot, garnished with fresh basil leaves.

Nutritional Values (per serving):

- Calories: 220 kcal
- Protein: 10g
- Carbohydrates: 38g
- Dietary Fiber: 12g
- Sugars: 10g
- Fat: 4.5g
- Saturated Fat: 0.5g
- Cholesterol: 0mg
- Sodium: 520mg

Why it's Nutrient-Rich for a Low-Nickel Lifestyle:

- **Tomatoes, Onion, Garlic, Basil:** As in the Classic Roasted Tomato Basil Soup.

- **Brown Lentils:** A low-nickel protein and fiber source.

- **Vegetable Broth:** Specifically chosen for its low-nickel content, providing a safe base.

5. Tomato Basil Quinoa Soup

Ingredients:

- 1/2 cup quinoa, rinsed

- 4 cups low-nickel vegetable broth

- 8 cups tomatoes, diced

- 1 large onion, diced

- 4 cloves garlic, minced

- 2 tablespoons olive oil

- Salt and pepper to taste

- 1 cup fresh basil leaves, chopped

- 1 teaspoon dried rosemary

- Fresh basil leaves for garnish

Instructions:

1. In a pot, combine quinoa and low-nickel vegetable broth. Bring to a boil, then reduce heat and simmer for 15-20 minutes or until quinoa is cooked.

2. In a separate pan, sauté diced onion and minced garlic in olive oil until softened.

3. Add diced tomatoes to the pan and cook until they release their juices.

4. Combine the quinoa mixture with the sautéed vegetables.

5. Season with salt, pepper, fresh basil, and dried rosemary.

6. Simmer for an additional 10-15 minutes.

7. Adjust seasoning if needed.

8. Serve hot, garnished with fresh basil leaves.

Nutritional Values (per serving):

- Calories: 240 kcal

- Protein: 8g

- Carbohydrates: 42g

- Dietary Fiber: 9g

- Sugars: 12g

- Fat: 5g

- Saturated Fat: 0.5g

- Cholesterol: 0mg

- Sodium: 540mg

Why it's Nutrient-Rich for a Low-Nickel Lifestyle:

- **Tomatoes, Onion, Garlic, Basil:** As in the Classic Roasted Tomato Basil Soup.

- **Quinoa:** A low-nickel grain providing protein, fiber, and essential amino acids.

- **Vegetable Broth:** Specifically chosen for its low-nickel content, providing a safe base.

These 'Roasted Tomato Basil Soup' variations are crafted with careful consideration of a low-nickel lifestyle. Each recipe not only adheres to dietary restrictions but also offers a rich array of nutrients from fresh, wholesome ingredients, making them not just nourishing but also delightful to the palate.

Ginger Turmeric Lentil Stew

1. Classic Ginger Turmeric Lentil Stew

Ingredients:

- 1 cup brown lentils, rinsed
- 6 cups low-nickel vegetable broth
- 1 large onion, diced
- 4 carrots, sliced
- 3 celery stalks, chopped
- 4 cloves garlic, minced
- 2 tablespoons fresh ginger, grated
- 1 tablespoon ground turmeric
- 1 teaspoon ground cumin
- 1 teaspoon paprika
- Salt and pepper to taste
- 1 can (14 oz) diced tomatoes
- 1 cup kale, chopped
- Fresh cilantro for garnish

Instructions:

1. In a pot, combine brown lentils and low-nickel vegetable broth. Bring to a boil, then reduce heat and simmer for 25-30 minutes or until lentils are tender.

2. In a separate pan, sauté diced onion, sliced carrots, and chopped celery until softened.

3. Add minced garlic, grated ginger, ground turmeric, cumin, paprika, salt, and pepper. Sauté for an additional 2-3 minutes.

4. Combine the sautéed vegetables with the lentil mixture in the pot.

5. Add diced tomatoes and chopped kale.

6. Simmer for an additional 10-15 minutes.

7. Adjust seasoning if needed.

8. Serve hot, garnished with fresh cilantro.

Nutritional Values (per serving):

- Calories: 250 kcal
- Protein: 15g
- Carbohydrates: 45g
- Dietary Fiber: 15g
- Sugars: 8g
- Fat: 2.5g
- Saturated Fat: 0.5g
- Cholesterol: 0mg
- Sodium: 650mg

Why it's Nutrient-Rich for a Low-Nickel Lifestyle:

- **Brown Lentils:** A low-nickel protein and fiber source.
- **Vegetables (Onion, Carrots, Celery, Garlic, Kale):** Nutrient-dense without high nickel levels.
- **Ginger and Turmeric:** Anti-inflammatory properties without significant nickel content.

- **Tomatoes:** A low-nickel fruit high in vitamins A and C.

2. Coconut Ginger Turmeric Lentil Stew

Ingredients:

- 1 cup brown lentils, rinsed
- 6 cups low-nickel coconut milk
- 1 large onion, diced
- 4 carrots, sliced
- 3 celery stalks, chopped
- 4 cloves garlic, minced
- 2 tablespoons fresh ginger, grated
- 1 tablespoon ground turmeric
- 1 teaspoon ground cumin
- 1 teaspoon paprika
- Salt and pepper to taste
- 1 can (14 oz) diced tomatoes
- 1 cup kale, chopped
- Fresh cilantro and coconut flakes for garnish

Instructions:

1. In a pot, combine brown lentils and low-nickel coconut milk. Bring to a boil, then reduce heat and simmer for 25-30 minutes or until lentils are tender.

2. In a separate pan, sauté diced onion, sliced carrots, and chopped celery until softened.

3. Add minced garlic, grated ginger, ground turmeric, cumin, paprika, salt, and pepper. Sauté for an additional 2-3 minutes.

4. Combine the sautéed vegetables with the lentil mixture in the pot.

5. Add diced tomatoes and chopped kale.

6. Simmer for an additional 10-15 minutes.

7. Adjust seasoning if needed.

8. Serve hot, garnished with fresh cilantro and coconut flakes.

Nutritional Values (per serving):

- Calories: 280 kcal
- Protein: 14g
- Carbohydrates: 38g
- Dietary Fiber: 11g
- Sugars: 6g
- Fat: 10g
- Saturated Fat: 7g
- Cholesterol: 0mg
- Sodium: 530mg

Why it's Nutrient-Rich for a Low-Nickel Lifestyle:

- **Brown Lentils:** A low-nickel protein and fiber source.

- **Vegetables (Onion, Carrots, Celery, Garlic, Kale):** Nutrient-dense without high nickel levels.

- **Coconut Milk:** Adds creaminess and healthy fats for those less sensitive to nickel.

- **Ginger and Turmeric:** Anti-inflammatory properties without significant nickel content.

- **Tomatoes:** A low-nickel fruit high in vitamins A and C.

3. Lemon Ginger Turmeric Lentil Stew

Ingredients:

- 1 cup brown lentils, rinsed
- 6 cups low-nickel vegetable broth
- 1 large onion, diced
- 4 carrots, sliced
- 3 celery stalks, chopped
- 4 cloves garlic, minced
- 2 tablespoons fresh ginger, grated
- 1 tablespoon ground turmeric
- 1 teaspoon ground cumin
- 1 teaspoon paprika
- Salt and pepper to taste
- Juice of 2 lemons
- 1 can (14 oz) diced tomatoes
- 1 cup kale, chopped
- Fresh parsley for garnish

Instructions:

1. In a pot, combine brown lentils and low-nickel vegetable broth. Bring to a boil, then reduce heat and simmer for 25-30 minutes or until lentils are tender.

2. In a separate pan, sauté diced onion, sliced carrots, and chopped celery until softened.

3. Add minced garlic, grated ginger, ground turmeric, cumin, paprika, salt, and pepper. Sauté for an additional 2-3 minutes.

4. Combine the sautéed vegetables with the lentil mixture in the pot.

5. Add diced tomatoes and chopped kale.

6. Simmer for an additional 10-15 minutes.

7. Adjust seasoning if needed.

8. Stir in the juice of 2 lemons.

9. Serve hot, garnished with fresh parsley.

Nutritional Values (per serving):

- Calories: 240 kcal
- Protein: 13g
- Carbohydrates: 42g
- Dietary Fiber: 14g
- Sugars: 7g
- Fat: 2.5g
- Saturated Fat: 0.5g
- Cholesterol: 0mg
- Sodium: 640mg

Why it's Nutrient-Rich for a Low-Nickel Lifestyle:

- **Brown Lentils:** A low-nickel protein and fiber source.

- **Vegetables (Onion, Carrots, Celery, Garlic, Kale):** Nutrient-dense without high nickel levels.

- **Ginger and Turmeric:** Anti-inflammatory properties without significant nickel content.

- **Lemon Juice:** Adds a citrusy flavor without contributing to nickel sensitivity.

- **Tomatoes:** A low-nickel fruit high in vitamins A and C.

4. Moroccan Spiced Ginger Turmeric Lentil Stew

Ingredients:

- 1 cup brown lentils, rinsed
- 6 cups low-nickel vegetable broth
- 1 large onion, diced
- 4 carrots, sliced
- 3 celery stalks, chopped
- 4 cloves garlic, minced
- 2 tablespoons fresh ginger, grated
- 1 tablespoon ground turmeric
- 1 teaspoon ground cumin
- 1 teaspoon coriander
- 1 teaspoon cinnamon
- Salt and pepper to taste
- 1 can (14 oz) diced tomatoes
- 1 cup kale, chopped
- Fresh cilantro for garnish

Instructions:

1. In a pot, combine brown lentils and low-nickel vegetable broth. Bring to a boil, then reduce heat and simmer for 25-30 minutes or until lentils are tender.

2. In a separate pan, sauté diced onion, sliced carrots, and chopped celery until softened.

3. Add minced garlic, grated ginger, ground turmeric, cumin, coriander, cinnamon, salt, and pepper. Sauté for an additional 2-3 minutes.

4. Combine the sautéed vegetables with the lentil mixture in the pot.

5. Add diced tomatoes and chopped kale.

6. Simmer for an additional 10-15 minutes.

7. Adjust seasoning if needed.

8. Serve hot, garnished with fresh cilantro.

Nutritional Values (per serving):

- Calories: 260 kcal
- Protein: 14g
- Carbohydrates: 45g
- Dietary Fiber: 13g
- Sugars: 7g
- Fat: 2.5g
- Saturated Fat: 0.5g
- Cholesterol: 0mg
- Sodium: 620mg

Why it's Nutrient-Rich for a Low-Nickel Lifestyle:

- **Brown Lentils:** A low-nickel protein and fiber source.

- **Vegetables (Onion, Carrots, Celery, Garlic, Kale):** Nutrient-dense without high nickel levels.

- **Ginger and Turmeric:** Anti-inflammatory properties without significant nickel content.

- **Spices (Cumin, Coriander, Cinnamon):** Add flavor without contributing to nickel sensitivity.

- **Tomatoes:** A low-nickel fruit high in vitamins A and C.

5. Thai Coconut Ginger Turmeric Lentil Stew

Ingredients:

- 1 cup brown lentils, rinsed

- 6 cups low-nickel coconut milk

- 1 large onion, diced

- 4 carrots, sliced

- 3 celery stalks, chopped

- 4 cloves garlic, minced

- 2 tablespoons fresh ginger, grated

- 1 tablespoon ground turmeric

- 1 teaspoon red curry paste

- Salt and pepper to taste

- 1 can (14 oz) diced tomatoes

- 1 cup bok choy, chopped

- Fresh cilantro and lime wedges for garnish

Instructions:

1. In a pot, combine brown lentils and low-nickel coconut milk. Bring to a boil, then reduce heat and simmer for 25-30 minutes or until lentils are tender.

2. In a separate pan, sauté diced onion, sliced carrots, and chopped celery until softened.

3. Add minced garlic, grated ginger, ground turmeric, red curry paste, salt, and pepper. Sauté for an additional 2-3 minutes.

4. Combine the sautéed vegetables with the lentil mixture in the pot.

5. Add diced tomatoes and chopped bok choy.

6. Simmer for an additional 10-15 minutes.

7. Adjust seasoning if needed.

8. Serve hot, garnished with fresh cilantro and lime wedges.

Nutritional Values (per serving):

- Calories: 290 kcal
- Protein: 13g
- Carbohydrates: 38g
- Dietary Fiber: 11g
- Sugars: 7g
- Fat: 12g
- Saturated Fat: 9g
- Cholesterol: 0mg
- Sodium: 580mg

Why it's Nutrient-Rich for a Low-Nickel Lifestyle:

- **Brown Lentils:** A low-nickel protein and fiber source.

- **Vegetables (Onion, Carrots, Celery, Bok Choy):** Nutrient-dense without high nickel levels.

- **Coconut Milk:** Adds creaminess and healthy fats for those less sensitive to nickel.

- **Ginger and Turmeric:** Anti-inflammatory properties without significant nickel content.

- **Tomatoes:** A low-nickel fruit high in vitamins A and C.

These 'Ginger Turmeric Lentil Stew' variations are carefully crafted to align with the principles of a low-nickel lifestyle. Each recipe offers a harmonious blend of flavors and nutrients, ensuring a satisfying and nourishing experience for those navigating nickel sensitivities.

Coconut Curry Delight

Ingredients:

- 1 cup chickpeas, cooked
- 2 cups low-nickel coconut milk
- 1 large onion, diced
- 3 bell peppers (mix of colors), sliced
- 1 cup broccoli florets
- 4 cloves garlic, minced
- 2 tablespoons fresh ginger, grated
- 2 tablespoons curry powder
- 1 teaspoon turmeric
- Salt and pepper to taste
- 1 tablespoon coconut oil
- Fresh cilantro for garnish

Instructions:

1. In a pan, heat coconut oil over medium heat. Add diced onion and sauté until translucent.

2. Add minced garlic, grated ginger, curry powder, turmeric, salt, and pepper. Sauté for an additional 2-3 minutes.

3. Add sliced bell peppers and broccoli florets. Cook until vegetables are tender.

4. Pour in low-nickel coconut milk and add cooked chickpeas. Simmer for 10-15 minutes.

5. Adjust seasoning if needed.

6. Serve hot, garnished with fresh cilantro.

Nutritional Values (per serving):

- Calories: 280 kcal
- Protein: 10g
- Carbohydrates: 35g
- Dietary Fiber: 8g
- Sugars: 8g
- Fat: 12g
- Saturated Fat: 9g
- Cholesterol: 0mg
- Sodium: 480mg

Why it's Nutrient-Rich for a Low-Nickel Lifestyle:

- **Chickpeas:** A low-nickel protein source.
- **Vegetables (Onion, Bell Peppers, Broccoli):** Nutrient-dense without high nickel levels.
- **Coconut Milk:** Adds creaminess and healthy fats for those less sensitive to nickel.
- **Spices (Curry Powder, Turmeric):** Add flavor without contributing to nickel sensitivity.

2. Thai Basil Coconut Curry Delight

Ingredients:

- 1 cup tofu, cubed
- 2 cups low-nickel coconut milk
- 1 large onion, sliced
- 1 red bell pepper, sliced
- 1 yellow bell pepper, sliced
- 1 cup snap peas
- 4 cloves garlic, minced
- 2 tablespoons fresh basil, chopped
- 2 tablespoons red curry paste
- 1 tablespoon soy sauce
- Salt and pepper to taste
- 1 tablespoon coconut oil
- Fresh cilantro for garnish

Instructions:

1. In a pan, heat coconut oil over medium heat. Add sliced onion and sauté until golden brown.
2. Add minced garlic, red curry paste, soy sauce, salt, and pepper. Sauté for an additional 2-3 minutes.
3. Add cubed tofu and cook until lightly browned.
4. Add sliced bell peppers and snap peas. Cook until vegetables are tender.
5. Pour in low-nickel coconut milk and add fresh basil. Simmer for 10-15 minutes.
6. Adjust seasoning if needed.

7. Serve hot, garnished with fresh cilantro.

Nutritional Values (per serving):

- Calories: 320 kcal
- Protein: 14g
- Carbohydrates: 28g
- Dietary Fiber: 7g
- Sugars: 6g
- Fat: 18g
- Saturated Fat: 14g
- Cholesterol: 0mg
- Sodium: 560mg

Why it's Nutrient-Rich for a Low-Nickel Lifestyle:

- **Tofu:** A low-nickel protein source.
- **Vegetables (Onion, Bell Peppers, Snap Peas):** Nutrient-dense without high nickel levels.
- **Coconut Milk:** Adds creaminess and healthy fats for those less sensitive to nickel.
- **Basil and Red Curry Paste:** Add flavor without contributing to nickel sensitivity.

3. Lemongrass Coconut Curry Delight

Ingredients:

- 1 cup shrimp, peeled and deveined
- 2 cups low-nickel coconut milk
- 1 large onion, diced
- 2 carrots, sliced
- 1 zucchini, sliced
- 4 cloves garlic, minced
- 2 tablespoons lemongrass, finely chopped
- 1 tablespoon yellow curry powder
- Salt and pepper to taste
- 1 tablespoon coconut oil
- Fresh cilantro for garnish

Instructions:

1. In a pan, heat coconut oil over medium heat. Add diced onion and sauté until translucent.

2. Add minced garlic, chopped lemongrass, yellow curry powder, salt, and pepper. Sauté for an additional 2-3 minutes.

3. Add shrimp and cook until pink and opaque.

4. Add sliced carrots and zucchini. Cook until vegetables are tender.

5. Pour in low-nickel coconut milk. Simmer for 10-15 minutes.

6. Adjust seasoning if needed.

7. Serve hot, garnished with fresh cilantro.

Nutritional Values (per serving):

- Calories: 280 kcal
- Protein: 18g
- Carbohydrates: 24g
- Dietary Fiber: 6g
- Sugars: 8g
- Fat: 14g
- Saturated Fat: 11g
- Cholesterol: 90mg
- Sodium: 520mg

Why it's Nutrient-Rich for a Low-Nickel Lifestyle:

- **Shrimp:** A low-nickel protein source.
- **Vegetables (Onion, Carrots, Zucchini):** Nutrient-dense without high nickel levels.
- **Coconut Milk:** Adds creaminess and healthy fats for those less sensitive to nickel.
- **Lemongrass:** Adds citrusy flavor without contributing to nickel sensitivity.

4. Vegetable Medley Coconut Curry Delight

Ingredients:

- 1 cup mixed vegetables (broccoli, cauliflower, carrots), chopped
- 2 cups low-nickel coconut milk
- 1 large onion, diced
- 1 cup mushrooms, sliced
- 4 cloves garlic, minced
- 1 tablespoon curry powder
- 1 teaspoon ground coriander
- Salt and pepper to taste
- 1 tablespoon coconut oil
- Fresh parsley for garnish

Instructions:

1. In a pan, heat coconut oil over medium heat. Add diced onion and sauté until golden brown.

2. Add minced garlic, curry powder, ground coriander, salt, and pepper. Sauté for an additional 2-3 minutes.

3. Add mixed vegetables and sliced mushrooms. Cook until vegetables are tender.

4. Pour in low-nickel coconut milk. Simmer for 10-15 minutes.

5. Adjust seasoning if needed.

6. Serve hot, garnished with fresh parsley.

Nutritional Values (per serving):

- Calories: 250 kcal
- Protein: 8g
- Carbohydrates: 20g
- Dietary Fiber: 5g
- Sugars: 6g
- Fat: 16g
- Saturated Fat: 12g
- Cholesterol: 0mg
- Sodium: 480mg

Why it's Nutrient-Rich for a Low-Nickel Lifestyle:

- **Mixed Vegetables (Broccoli, Cauliflower, Carrots, Mushrooms):** Nutrient-dense without high nickel levels.

- **Coconut Milk:** Adds creaminess and healthy fats for those less sensitive to nickel.

- **Spices (Curry Powder, Coriander):** Add flavor without contributing to nickel sensitivity.

5. Lentil Coconut Curry Delight

Ingredients:

- 1 cup red lentils, rinsed
- 2 cups low-nickel coconut milk
- 1 large onion, diced
- 1 sweet potato, diced
- 1 cup spinach, chopped
- 4 cloves garlic, minced
- 1 tablespoon curry powder
- 1 teaspoon ground cumin
- Salt and pepper to taste
- 1 tablespoon coconut oil
- Fresh cilantro for garnish

Instructions:

1. In a pan, heat coconut oil over medium heat. Add diced onion and sauté until translucent.
2. Add minced garlic, curry powder, ground cumin, salt, and pepper. Sauté for an additional 2-3 minutes.
3. Add diced sweet potato and red lentils. Cook for 5 minutes.
4. Pour in low-nickel coconut milk and simmer for 20-25 minutes or until lentils and sweet potatoes are tender.
5. Add chopped spinach and cook until wilted.
6. Adjust seasoning if needed.
7. Serve hot, garnished with fresh cilantro.

Nutritional Values (per serving):

- Calories: 290 kcal
- Protein: 12g
- Carbohydrates: 38g
- Dietary Fiber: 10g
- Sugars: 6g
- Fat: 10g
- Saturated Fat: 7g
- Cholesterol: 0mg
- Sodium: 540mg

Why it's Nutrient-Rich for a Low-Nickel Lifestyle:

- **Red Lentils:** A low-nickel protein and fiber source.
- **Vegetables (Onion, Sweet Potato, Spinach):** Nutrient-dense without high nickel levels.
- **Coconut Milk:** Adds creaminess and healthy fats for those less sensitive to nickel.
- **Spices (Curry Powder, Cumin):** Add flavor without contributing to nickel sensitivity.

These 'Coconut Curry Delight' recipes are thoughtfully designed to cater to the nutritional needs of individuals following a low-nickel lifestyle. Each variation combines vibrant flavors with nutrient-rich ingredients, ensuring a delightful culinary experience that aligns with the principles of a low-nickel diet.

CHAPTER EIGHT
MASTERING THE NICKEL CHALLENGE

The Art of Portion Control

In the culinary journey outlined in the "Low Nickel Diet Cookbook for Beginners," the art of portion control emerges as a cornerstone in achieving a harmonious balance between delectable flavors and mindful nourishment. Within the context of a low-nickel lifestyle, mastering the art of portion control takes on added significance, offering a nuanced approach that enhances both culinary experiences and overall well-being.

1. Mindful Enjoyment of Low-Nickel Delights: In the realm of low-nickel culinary creations, the art of portion control encourages individuals to savor every bite intentionally. It invites a mindful appreciation for the carefully crafted recipes presented in the cookbook, allowing readers to indulge in the delightful flavors without compromising their dietary goals.

2. Balancing Nutrient-Rich Offerings: The low-nickel lifestyle, as advocated in the cookbook, emphasizes the inclusion of nutrient-dense ingredients. The art of portion control aligns seamlessly with this principle, guiding individuals to create well-balanced meals that not only address nickel sensitivity but also provide a rich array of essential nutrients vital for vibrant health.

3. Tailoring Portions to Individual Needs: Recognizing that every person has unique dietary requirements, the art of portion control in the low-nickel context encourages a personalized approach. It empowers individuals to customize their serving sizes based on factors such as age, activity level, and personal preferences, ensuring a sustainable and satisfying culinary experience.

4. Culinary Creativity in Portion Presentation: The cookbook's emphasis on whole foods and mindful ingredients finds synergy with the art of portion control. It inspires culinary creativity by encouraging individuals to explore diverse textures, vibrant colors, and appealing presentations. Meals become not only a source of nourishment but also a feast for the senses.

5. Practical Strategies for Low-Nickel Living: As individuals embark on the low-nickel journey, practical strategies for portion control become invaluable. The art of portion control, as woven into the fabric of the cookbook, provides readers with actionable insights and tools for adapting portion control strategies to various settings, be it home-cooked meals, dining out, or social gatherings.

6. Sustaining a Lifelong Connection with Health: Embracing the art of portion control within the low-nickel lifestyle extends beyond short-term dietary adjustments. It fosters a sustainable and adaptable approach to health, encouraging individuals to view their well-being as a lifelong journey. This philosophy aligns seamlessly with the cookbook's message of empowering individuals to take control of their dietary needs for a fulfilling and enduring life.

In essence, the "Low Nickel Diet Cookbook For Beginners" becomes not just a collection of recipes but a guide that seamlessly integrates the art of portion control into the fabric of a low-nickel lifestyle. It empowers individuals to approach their culinary journey with intention, fostering a profound connection with their dietary choices and paving the way for a healthier, more vibrant future.

Savvy Strategies for Socializing

Navigating social events while adhering to a low-nickel lifestyle can present unique challenges, but with a thoughtful and strategic approach, individuals can not only maintain their dietary needs but also enjoy meaningful social connections. The "Low Nickel Diet Cookbook For Beginners" extends its guidance beyond the kitchen, offering savvy strategies for socializing that empower individuals to confidently engage in a variety of social settings.

1. **Communication is Key:** Open and honest communication forms the foundation of successful socializing within the low-nickel lifestyle. Informing friends, family, and hosts about dietary restrictions helps create an understanding and fosters an environment where everyone can enjoy the gathering.

2. **Potluck Power:** When attending social events, suggest a potluck-style gathering where each attendee contributes a dish. This not only ensures that there are low-nickel options available but also allows individuals to showcase their culinary creations from the cookbook, promoting a shared experience.

3. **Mastering the Art of Label Reading:** Whether at a friend's house or a restaurant, mastering the art of reading food labels becomes a valuable skill. The cookbook equips individuals with knowledge about nickel content in various foods, empowering them to make informed choices and enjoy social occasions without compromising their dietary needs.

4. **Preparing Grab-and-Go Snacks:** For spontaneous social gatherings or events where food options might be limited, the cookbook offers recipes for easy-to-prepare grab-and-go snacks. Having a stash of these snacks ensures that

individuals can indulge in socializing without worrying about finding suitable food.

5. **Hosting Low-Nickel Dinners:** Taking the reins as a host provides the opportunity to curate a menu that aligns with the low-nickel lifestyle. The cookbook guides readers in crafting delightful meals that cater to guests with diverse dietary needs, fostering an inclusive and enjoyable social experience.

6. **Savoring Non-Food Social Activities:** The cookbook encourages individuals to broaden their definition of socializing beyond just food-centric events. Engaging in activities such as hiking, game nights, or art gatherings allows for meaningful connections without the primary focus on food.

7. **Building a Supportive Network:** Connecting with others who share similar dietary challenges can be immensely beneficial. The cookbook promotes the idea of building a supportive network where individuals can exchange tips, share experiences, and provide encouragement, creating a sense of camaraderie.

8. **Crafting Low-Nickel Cocktails:** Socializing often involves drinks, and the cookbook extends its expertise to crafting low-nickel cocktails. These refreshing beverages not only align with dietary restrictions but also add a touch of flair to social events.

9. **Embracing Flexibility:** The art of socializing within the low-nickel lifestyle involves embracing flexibility. While adhering to dietary guidelines is crucial, maintaining a balanced perspective allows individuals to enjoy social occasions without unnecessary stress.

10. **Celebrating Achievements:** The cookbook encourages individuals to celebrate their achievements in navigating

social situations while adhering to a low-nickel lifestyle. Every successfully managed gathering is a triumph, and recognizing these victories fosters a positive and empowered mindset.

In summary, the "Low Nickel Diet Cookbook for Beginners" not only provides delectable recipes but also equips individuals with savvy strategies for socializing. By fostering open communication, embracing flexibility, and offering practical tips for various scenarios, the cookbook becomes a valuable companion in navigating the social landscape with confidence and enjoyment.

Dining out with Distinction: Navigating Low-Nickel Options with Confidence

In the world of low nickel living, the sub-chapter "Dining Out with Distinction" from the "Low Nickel Diet Cookbook For Beginners" serves as a comprehensive guide to empower individuals in maintaining their dietary needs while enjoying restaurant experiences. This section offers practical insights, strategic tips, and savvy approaches to navigating restaurant menus with confidence and distinction.

1. Understanding Menu Language: The sub-chapter begins by unravelling the nuances of menu language. It educates readers on common terms and phrases that may indicate nickel-rich ingredients, enabling them to make informed choices when perusing restaurant menus.

2. Strategic Restaurant Selection: Dining out becomes an enjoyable experience when individuals strategically choose restaurants that align with their low-nickel dietary goals. The sub-chapter provides guidance on selecting eateries known for their diverse, fresh, and customizable options, enhancing the chances of finding suitable dishes.

3. Open Communication with Servers: An integral aspect of dining out with a low-nickel distinction involves open communication with restaurant staff. The cookbook advises readers on effectively communicating their dietary restrictions to servers, fostering a collaborative effort to create a dining experience that meets individual needs.

4. Customizing Orders for Low-Nickel Living: The sub-chapter delves into the art of customizing menu items to suit low-nickel requirements. It encourages readers to confidently request modifications, substitutions, or exclusions, ensuring that each dish aligns with their dietary preferences without compromising on flavor.

5. Spotlight on Whole Foods: Recognizing that whole foods play a pivotal role in low nickel living, the sub-chapter directs attention to menu items that prominently feature fresh fruits, vegetables, and lean proteins. It empowers individuals to make choices that not only adhere to dietary restrictions but also prioritize nutritional value.

6. Navigating Culinary Cuisines: The world of culinary cuisines offers a rich tapestry of flavors, and the sub-chapter guides readers through navigating various cuisines while adhering to low-nickel principles. From Mediterranean delights to Asian-inspired dishes, individuals learn how to appreciate diverse flavors without compromising their dietary needs.

7. Pre-Planning for Dining Success: Success in dining out with distinction often involves pre-planning. The sub-chapter provides practical tips for researching restaurant menus in advance, enabling individuals to enter dining establishments with a clear plan and an understanding of low-nickel options available.

8. Celebrating Culinary Triumphs: The sub-chapter concludes by emphasizing the importance of celebrating culinary triumphs. Every successfully navigated restaurant experience is a victory, and the cookbook encourages individuals to acknowledge and celebrate these achievements as they gain confidence in their ability to dine out with distinction.

In essence, "Dining Out with Distinction" in the context of the "Low Nickel Diet Cookbook for Beginners" becomes a beacon of empowerment. It equips individuals with the knowledge, strategies, and confidence needed to not only enjoy restaurant experiences but also to do so with distinction, savoring the delights of the culinary world while prioritizing their low-nickel dietary lifestyle.

CHAPTER NINE
BEYOND THE PLATE
Integrating Whole Foods And Mindful Ingredients

A key cornerstone of the "Low Nickel Diet Cookbook for Beginners" is the emphasis on whole foods and mindful ingredients. This approach not only aligns with the principles of a low-nickel diet but also promotes overall health and well-being. Let's delve into the detailed steps of how to seamlessly integrate whole foods and mindful ingredients into a low-nickel lifestyle:

1. **Understanding Whole Foods:** Whole foods refer to minimally processed, unrefined, and nutrient-dense ingredients in their natural state. In the context of a low-nickel diet, focusing on whole foods ensures that individuals consume fresh, wholesome ingredients with minimal risk of nickel contamination.

2. **Embracing Fresh Fruits and Vegetables:** The cookbook encourages the incorporation of fresh fruits and vegetables, emphasizing those with lower nickel content. Leafy greens, berries, apples, and pears are often recommended choices. These nutrient-rich options not only provide essential vitamins and minerals but also contribute to a varied and flavorful diet.

3. **Prioritizing Lean Proteins:** Whole, lean protein sources play a crucial role in a low-nickel diet. Opting for sources such as poultry, fish, eggs, and legumes provides ample protein while minimizing nickel exposure. The cookbook offers diverse recipes that showcase these proteins in delicious and creative ways.

4. **Choosing Whole Grains:** Whole grains are a rich source of fiber, vitamins, and minerals. In a low-nickel diet,

selecting grains like brown rice, quinoa, and oats ensures a nutrient-dense foundation for meals. The cookbook provides a variety of recipes that incorporate these whole grains, contributing to both flavor and nutritional value.

5. Incorporating Mindful Ingredients: Mindful ingredients, as advocated in the cookbook, involve selecting items consciously, considering their nutritional profile and potential nickel content. This includes scrutinizing labels, opting for fresh produce, and choosing minimally processed items. Mindful ingredients contribute to a cleaner, more health-conscious approach to cooking.

6. Avoiding Nickel-Rich Processed Foods: Processed foods are often culprits for hidden nickel content. The cookbook guides individuals to steer clear of processed and canned goods, opting instead for fresh alternatives. This proactive approach minimizes the risk of unintentional nickel exposure, aligning with the principles of a low-nickel lifestyle.

7. Crafting Balanced and Flavorful Meals: Integrating whole foods and mindful ingredients is not about sacrifice but about crafting balanced, flavorful meals. The cookbook's recipes are designed to showcase the vibrant and diverse flavors of whole foods, ensuring that individuals enjoy their culinary journey while adhering to a low-nickel diet.

8. Exploring Culinary Creativity: The cookbook encourages readers to explore culinary creativity within the realm of whole foods. From unique spice blends to innovative cooking techniques, individuals can elevate their dishes while staying true to the principles of a low-nickel lifestyle.

9. Prioritizing Nutrient Density: Whole foods are inherently nutrient-dense, providing a wealth of essential vitamins and minerals. The cookbook emphasizes the importance of prioritizing nutrient density, ensuring that each meal contributes to overall health and vitality.

10. Celebrating the Joy of Whole Food Cooking: Finally, the cookbook fosters a celebration of the joy of whole food cooking. It promotes a positive and fulfilling culinary experience, where individuals can savor the delights of fresh, wholesome ingredients while nurturing their bodies on their low-nickel journey.

In conclusion, integrating whole foods and mindful ingredients into a low-nickel diet is a holistic and enriching approach. The "Low Nickel Diet Cookbook for Beginners" serves as a guide, offering not just recipes but a philosophy that empowers individuals to embrace a health-conscious and flavorful culinary lifestyle within the bounds of a low-nickel diet.

Fresh Produce: Your Allies In Health

In the context of the "Low Nickel Diet Cookbook For Beginners," the section on "Fresh Produce: Your Allies in Health" highlights the vital role that fruits and vegetables play in maintaining well-being, especially for those adhering to a low-nickel diet. Let's explore the significance and benefits of incorporating fresh produce as allies in health:

1. **Abundant in Essential Nutrients:** Fresh produce, including a variety of fruits and vegetables, is abundant in essential nutrients such as vitamins, minerals, and antioxidants. These nutrients are crucial for supporting overall health, bolstering the immune system, and promoting optimal bodily functions.

2. **Low in Nickel Content:** The cookbook underscores the importance of choosing fresh produce with low nickel content. Certain fruits and vegetables, such as leafy greens, berries, apples, and pears, are recommended for their minimal nickel levels. This ensures that individuals can enjoy the nutritional benefits of fresh produce without compromising their low-nickel dietary goals.

3. **Rich in Dietary Fiber:** Fresh produce is an excellent source of dietary fiber, which is essential for digestive health. Fiber aids in maintaining bowel regularity, promoting a healthy gut microbiome, and supporting weight management. The cookbook encourages the inclusion of a variety of fresh fruits and vegetables to enhance fiber intake.

4. **Variety for Flavorful Meals:** The diversity of fresh produce allows for the creation of flavorful and visually appealing meals. The cookbook provides a range of recipes that showcase the vibrant colors, textures, and tastes of different fruits and vegetables, making the low-nickel diet an enjoyable and satisfying culinary experience.

5. Hydration and Electrolyte Balance: Many fresh fruits and vegetables have high water content, contributing to hydration and electrolyte balance. This is particularly beneficial for individuals on a low-nickel diet, as proper hydration supports overall health and aids in the elimination of toxins from the body.

6. Antioxidant Properties: Fresh produce is rich in antioxidants, compounds that help combat oxidative stress and inflammation. The cookbook highlights the importance of including antioxidant-rich fruits and vegetables in the diet to promote cellular health and reduce the risk of chronic diseases.

7. Snacking with Nutrient-Dense Options: Incorporating fresh produce into snacks is a nutritious and satisfying way to curb hunger. The cookbook offers creative and easy-to-prepare snack recipes that feature a variety of fruits and vegetables, providing individuals with nutrient-dense options for between-meal cravings.

8. Supporting Overall Well-Being: By making fresh produce a cornerstone of the low-nickel diet, individuals not only adhere to dietary guidelines but also support their overall well-being. The vitamins, minerals, and phytonutrients found in fruits and vegetables contribute to enhanced energy levels, improved mood, and a strengthened immune system.

9. Cooking with Fresh Ingredients: The cookbook encourages individuals to cook with fresh ingredients, celebrating the flavors and nutritional benefits of unprocessed produce. This approach aligns with the philosophy of creating wholesome and delicious meals while navigating the constraints of a low-nickel lifestyle.

10. Adapting to Seasonal Availability: The section on fresh produce acknowledges the importance of adapting to seasonal availability. Embracing seasonal fruits and vegetables not only ensures optimal freshness and flavor but also provides variety throughout the year.

In summary, "Fresh Produce: Your Allies in Health" serves as a guide within the "Low Nickel Diet Cookbook For Beginners," emphasizing the integral role of fruits and vegetables in promoting health and flavor within the context of a low-nickel diet.

Nutrient-Dense Elements for Vibrant Living

Within the "Low Nickel Diet Cookbook for Beginners," the section on "Nutrient-Dense Elements for Vibrant Living" is a comprehensive exploration of the essential components that contribute to overall health and vitality. This segment not only aligns with the principles of a low-nickel diet but also serves as a holistic guide to nourishing the body with the vital nutrients it needs. Let's delve into the detailed explanation of the nutrient-dense elements that foster vibrant living:

1. Essential Vitamins: Nutrient density begins with a focus on essential vitamins—organic compounds vital for various physiological functions. The cookbook emphasizes incorporating a diverse range of fruits, vegetables, and other whole foods to ensure an ample supply of vitamins crucial for immune function, energy production, and overall well-being.

2. Minerals for Optimal Functioning: The inclusion of mineral-rich foods is highlighted as a cornerstone of nutrient density. Essential minerals such as calcium, magnesium, potassium, and iron play pivotal roles in bone health, muscle function, electrolyte balance, and oxygen transport. The cookbook offers recipes that strategically incorporate these minerals through whole food choices.

3. Antioxidants and Phytonutrients: Antioxidants and phytonutrients are showcased as powerful elements in promoting vibrant living. These compounds, found in colorful fruits and vegetables, combat oxidative stress, reduce inflammation, and contribute to cellular health. The cookbook encourages the consumption of a rainbow of produce to maximize antioxidant and phytonutrient intake.

4. Lean Proteins for Muscle Health: Lean proteins are essential for muscle health, and the cookbook provides a variety of recipes featuring sources such as poultry, fish, eggs, and legumes. These proteins not only contribute to muscle maintenance and repair but also aid in achieving a balanced and satisfying diet.

5. Omega-3 Fatty Acids for Brain and Heart Health: Nutrient density extends to incorporating omega-3 fatty acids, crucial for brain and heart health. The cookbook guides readers in selecting foods rich in omega-3s, such as fatty fish and flaxseeds, to support cognitive function and cardiovascular well-being.

6. Dietary Fiber for Digestive Wellness: A focus on dietary fiber emerges as a key element for vibrant living. Fiber, abundant in whole grains, fruits, and vegetables, supports digestive wellness, regulates blood sugar levels, and promotes a feeling of fullness. The cookbook integrates fiber-rich ingredients into recipes to enhance digestive health.

7. Hydration for Overall Vitality: Nutrient density extends to proper hydration, recognized as essential for overall vitality. The cookbook emphasizes the importance of adequate water intake and offers recipes that include hydrating elements, such as fruits with high water content, to support optimal bodily functions.

8. Balanced Macronutrients: The cookbook advocates for a balanced intake of macronutrients—proteins, carbohydrates, and fats. Achieving a harmonious balance ensures sustained energy levels, supports metabolic functions, and contributes to an overall sense of well-being.

9. Mindful Ingredient Choices: The section on nutrient-dense elements underscores the significance of mindful ingredient choices. It encourages individuals to select fresh, unprocessed, and wholesome foods, avoiding additives and preservatives that may compromise nutrient density.

10. Culinary Creativity and Nutrient-Rich Recipes: Nutrient-dense living is presented as a journey of culinary creativity. The cookbook serves as a guide for crafting recipes that not only adhere to low-nickel principles but also celebrate the flavors and nutritional richness of whole foods, making the journey towards vibrant living enjoyable and sustainable.

In essence, "Nutrient-Dense Elements for Vibrant Living" within the "Low Nickel Diet Cookbook for Beginners" becomes a comprehensive roadmap for individuals seeking not just a dietary guide but a holistic approach to nourishing the body for optimal health and vitality.

CHAPTER TEN
STRATEGIC MEAL PLANNING

Crafting your Culinary Calendar

Crafting a culinary calendar that aligns with low-nickel goals and transforms mealtime into a celebration of health and vibrant living involves a thoughtful and strategic approach. Here's a step-by-step guide to help you navigate this culinary journey:

1. Set Clear Dietary Goals: Begin by defining clear and achievable dietary goals. Consider your nickel intake targets, nutritional needs, and any specific health objectives. These goals will serve as the foundation for crafting a culinary calendar tailored to your well-being.

2. Create a Weekly Meal Planning Template: Develop a weekly meal planning template to provide structure and organization. Outline breakfast, lunch, dinner, and snacks for each day. Having a visual representation helps you balance variety and nutritional content throughout the week.

3. Integrate Cookbook Recipes: Utilize the recipes from the "Low Nickel Diet Cookbook for Beginners." Integrate a diverse range of recipes into your meal calendar, ensuring a mix of flavors and nutrients. Experiment with breakfast, lunch, dinner, and snack options to keep your culinary experience exciting.

4. Embrace Seasonal Ingredients: Embrace the seasonal bounty by incorporating fresh, seasonal ingredients into your meal planning. Seasonal produce not only adds variety and flavor but also maximizes nutritional benefits. Explore local markets to discover new and vibrant ingredients.

5. Consider Batch Cooking: Streamline your meal preparation by incorporating batch cooking into your routine. Prepare larger quantities of meals that can be stored and reheated throughout the week. This efficient approach saves time while ensuring a consistent supply of low-nickel, delicious dishes.

6. Plan Efficient Shopping Lists: Craft strategic shopping lists based on your weekly meal plan. This minimizes food waste, ensures you have all necessary ingredients, and streamlines your shopping experience. Focus on fresh produce, lean proteins, and whole grains while avoiding high-nickel items.

7. Address Dietary Restrictions: Consider any additional dietary restrictions or preferences you may have. Adapt recipes to suit your needs and explore alternative ingredients that align with both your low-nickel goals and your overall well-being.

8. Prioritize Nutrient Density: Prioritize nutrient-dense ingredients in your meal planning. Include a variety of colorful fruits and vegetables, lean proteins, whole grains, and healthy fats to ensure your meals are not only low in nickel but also rich in essential vitamins and minerals.

9. Celebrate Culinary Successes: Celebrate your culinary successes along the way. Acknowledge your achievements in sticking to your low-nickel goals, trying new recipes, and maintaining a healthy and vibrant lifestyle. Positive reinforcement contributes to a sustainable and positive relationship with food.

10. Stay Flexible and Enjoy the Journey: While planning is essential, stay flexible and embrace the joy of culinary exploration. Allow room for spontaneity and occasional indulgences. Enjoy the process of discovering new flavors and nourishing your body in a way that feels sustainable and vibrant.

Crafting a culinary calendar aligned with low-nickel goals is not just a practical endeavor; it's an opportunity to savor the journey of health and vibrant living. By combining thoughtful planning, culinary creativity, and a celebration of successes, you can transform mealtime into a nourishing and enjoyable experience that supports your well-being.

Let's create a sample culinary calendar based on the principles outlined in the explanation:

Sample Culinary Calendar For A Low-Nickel Lifestyle
Monday:

- *Breakfast:* Quinoa Breakfast Bowl (Recipe from the cookbook)
- *Lunch:* Mediterranean Chickpea Salad
- *Dinner:* Citrus Glazed Salmon with Roasted Sweet Potatoes

Tuesday:

- *Breakfast:* Oatmeal with Fresh Berries
- *Lunch:* Avocado Bliss Wrap with a side of Cherry Tomatoes
- *Dinner:* Thai Zoodle Bowl Extravaganza

Wednesday:

- *Breakfast:* Nutty Banana Pancakes (Recipe from the cookbook)
- *Lunch:* Harvest Stuffed Bell Peppers

- *Dinner:* Spiced Cauliflower Steaks with Quinoa

Thursday:

- *Breakfast:* Sunrise Smoothie Delight (Recipe from the cookbook)
- *Lunch:* Quinoa Salad with Mixed Greens
- *Dinner:* Culinary Magic for Evenings - Grilled Chicken with Roasted Vegetables

Friday:

- *Breakfast:* Whole Grain Toast with Almond Butter and Sliced Apples
- *Lunch:* Thai Zoodle Bowl Extravaganza leftovers
- *Dinner:* Nourishing Elixirs - Ginger Turmeric Lentil Stew

Saturday:

- *Breakfast:* Nutrient-Rich Green Smoothie
- *Lunch:* Mediterranean Chickpea Salad Wrap
- *Dinner:* Coconut Curry Delight with Brown Rice

Sunday:

- *Breakfast:* Nutty Banana Pancakes (Recipe from the cookbook)
- *Lunch:* Culinary Magic for Evenings - Spaghetti Squash with Tomato Basil Sauce
- *Dinner:* Savory Soups for the Soul - Roasted Tomato Basil Soup

Additional Considerations:

- *Snacks:* Fresh fruit, nuts, or a small serving of Greek yogurt

- *Beverages:* Hydrate with water, herbal teas, or infused water with citrus slices.

Weekly Goals:
- Embrace seasonal produce in each meal.

- Practice batch cooking for convenience and efficiency.

- Ensure a balance of lean proteins, whole grains, and nutrient-dense fruits and vegetables.

- Stay mindful of individual dietary restrictions and preferences.

Remember, this is just a sample, and you can customize your culinary calendar based on your preferences, seasonal availability, and nutritional needs. Enjoy the journey of crafting nourishing and delicious meals that align with your low-nickel goals and contribute to a vibrant and healthy lifestyle.

A 30+Day Meal Plan For Seamless Integration

Here's a 30-day meal plan for seamless integration, featuring recipes from "The Low-Nickel Diet Cookbook for Beginners":

Day 1:

- **Breakfast:** Quinoa Breakfast Bowl
- **Lunch:** Mediterranean Chickpea Salad
- **Dinner:** Citrus Glazed Salmon with Roasted Sweet Potatoes
- **Snacks:** Fresh fruit or a small handful of nuts

Day 2:

- **Breakfast:** Oatmeal with Fresh Berries
- **Lunch:** Avocado Bliss Wrap with a side of Cherry Tomatoes
- **Dinner:** Thai Zoodle Bowl Extravaganza
- **Snacks:** Nutty Banana Pancakes (Recipe from the cookbook)

Day 3:

- **Breakfast:** Sunrise Smoothie Delight
- **Lunch:** Harvest Stuffed Bell Peppers
- **Dinner:** Spiced Cauliflower Steaks with Quinoa
- **Snacks:** Whole Grain Toast with Almond Butter and Sliced Apples

Day 4:

- **Breakfast:** Nutty Banana Pancakes (Recipe from the cookbook)
- **Lunch:** Quinoa Salad with Mixed Greens
- **Dinner:** Grilled Chicken with Roasted Vegetables (Culinary Magic for Evenings)
- **Snacks:** Nutrient-Rich Green Smoothie

Day 5:

- **Breakfast:** Nutty Banana Pancakes
- **Lunch:** Spaghetti Squash with Tomato Basil Sauce (Culinary Magic for Evenings)
- **Dinner:** Roasted Tomato Basil Soup (Savory Soups for the Soul)
- **Snacks:** Fresh fruit or a small serving of Greek yogurt

Day 6:

- **Breakfast:** Nutty Banana
- **Lunch:** Mediterranean Chickpea Salad Wrap
- **Dinner:** Coconut Curry Delight with Brown Rice
- **Snacks:** Nutrient-Rich Green Smoothie

Day 7:

- **Breakfast:** Whole Grain Toast with Almond Butter and Sliced Apples
- **Lunch:** Culinary Magic for Evenings - Grilled Chicken with Roasted Vegetables
- **Dinner:** Savory Soups for the Soul - Ginger Turmeric Lentil Stew
- **Snacks:** Fresh fruit or a small handful of nuts

Day 8:

- **Breakfast:** Quinoa Breakfast Bowl
- **Lunch:** Mediterranean Chickpea Salad
- **Dinner:** Citrus Glazed Salmon with Roasted Sweet Potatoes
- **Snacks:** Fresh fruit or a small handful of nuts

Day 9:

- **Breakfast:** Oatmeal with Fresh Berries
- **Lunch:** Avocado Bliss Wrap with a side of Cherry Tomatoes
- **Dinner:** Thai Zoodle Bowl Extravaganza
- **Snacks:** Nutty Banana Pancakes

Day 10:

- **Breakfast:** Sunrise Smoothie Delight
- **Lunch:** Harvest Stuffed Bell Peppers
- **Dinner:** Spiced Cauliflower Steaks with Quinoa
- **Snacks:** Whole Grain Toast with Almond Butter and Sliced Apples

Day 11:

- **Breakfast:** Nutty Banana Pancakes
- **Lunch:** Quinoa Salad with Mixed Greens
- **Dinner:** Grilled Chicken with Roasted Vegetables
- **Snacks:** Nutrient-rich green Smoothie

Day 12:

- **Breakfast:** Nutty Banana Pancakes (Recipe from the cookbook)
- **Lunch:** Spaghetti Squash with Tomato Basil Sauce (Culinary Magic for Evenings)
- **Dinner:** Roasted Tomato Basil Soup (Savory Soups for the Soul)
- **Snacks:** Fresh fruit or a small serving of Greek yogurt

Day 13:

- **Breakfast:** Nutty Banana Pancakes
- **Lunch:** Mediterranean Chickpea Salad Wrap
- **Dinner:** Coconut Curry Delight with Brown Rice
- **Snacks:** Nutrient-rich green Smoothie

Day 14:

- **Breakfast:** Whole Grain Toast with Almond Butter and Sliced Apples
- **Lunch:** Culinary Magic for Evenings - Grilled Chicken with Roasted Vegetables
- **Dinner:** Savory Soups for the Soul - Ginger Turmeric Lentil Stew
- **Snacks:** Fresh fruit or a small handful of nuts

Day 15:

- **Breakfast:** Blueberry Buckwheat Pancakes
- **Lunch:** Spinach and Strawberry Salad with Balsamic Vinaigrette
- **Dinner:** Lemon Garlic Shrimp Stir-Fry with Brown Rice
- **Snacks:** Fresh Mango Slices

Day 16:

- **Breakfast:** Chia Seed Pudding with Mixed Berries
- **Lunch:** Lentil and Vegetable Wrap with Tahini Sauce
- **Dinner:** Baked Cod with Herbed Quinoa
- **Snacks:** Greek Yogurt Parfait with Almonds and Honey

Day 17:

- **Breakfast:** Apple Cinnamon Overnight Oats
- **Lunch:** Caprese Salad with Avocado
- **Dinner:** Zucchini Noodles with Pesto and Cherry Tomatoes
- **Snacks:** Roasted Chickpeas

Day 18:

- **Breakfast:** Sweet Potato and Kale Breakfast Hash
- **Lunch:** Chickpea and Vegetable Stew
- **Dinner:** Turkey and Vegetable Skewers with Quinoa
- **Snacks:** Sliced Papaya with Lime

Day 19:

- **Breakfast:** Almond Flour Banana Muffins
- **Lunch:** Greek Salad with Quinoa
- **Dinner:** Stir-Fried Tofu with Broccoli and Cashews
- **Snacks:** Carrot Sticks with Hummus

Day 20:

- **Breakfast:** Raspberry Chia Jam on Whole Grain Toast
- **Lunch:** Cucumber and Avocado Sushi Rolls

- **Dinner:** Grilled Eggplant and Tomato Stacks
- **Snacks:** Trail Mix with Dried Cranberries

Day 21:

- **Breakfast:** Pineapple Coconut Smoothie Bowl
- **Lunch:** Quinoa and Black Bean Bowl with Lime Dressing
- **Dinner:** Baked Chicken with Lemon and Herbs, served with Asparagus
- **Snacks:** Fresh Kiwi Slices

Day 22:

- **Breakfast:** Quinoa and Blueberry Breakfast Bowl
- **Lunch:** Spinach and Feta Stuffed Bell Peppers
- **Dinner:** Lemon Herb Baked Salmon with Roasted Brussels Sprouts
- **Snacks:** Apple Slices with Almond Butter

Day 23:

- **Breakfast:** Oat and Banana Pancakes
- **Lunch:** Greek Salad with Grilled Chicken
- **Dinner:** Spaghetti Squash with Tomato Basil Sauce
- **Snacks:** Greek Yogurt Parfait with Mixed Berries

Day 24:

- **Breakfast:** Mango Coconut Chia Pudding
- **Lunch:** Quinoa and Black Bean Wrap with Avocado
- **Dinner:** Baked Cod with Lemon and Dill, served with Quinoa

- **Snacks:** Trail Mix with Walnuts and Dried Cranberries

Day 25:

- **Breakfast:** Sweet Potato and Kale Frittata
- **Lunch:** Chickpea and Vegetable Stir-Fry
- **Dinner:** Grilled Shrimp Skewers with Zucchini Noodles
- **Snacks:** Sliced Cucumber with Hummus

Day 26:

- **Breakfast:** Almond Flour Banana
- **Lunch:** Caprese Salad with Balsamic Glaze
- **Dinner:** Quinoa-Stuffed Bell Peppers with Turkey
- **Snacks:** Fresh Pineapple Chunks

Day 27:

- **Breakfast:** Raspberry Almond Smoothie Bowl
- **Lunch:** Lentil and Vegetable Curry
- **Dinner:** Baked Chicken Breast with Herbed Quinoa
- **Snacks:** Greek Yogurt with Honey and Pistachios

Day 28:

- **Breakfast:** Apple Cinnamon Overnight Oats
- **Lunch:** Mediterranean Chickpea Salad Wrap
- **Dinner:** Grilled Vegetable and Brown Rice Bowl
- **Snacks:** Mixed Berries with a Dollop of Greek Yogurt

Day 29:

- **Breakfast:** Quinoa and Blueberry Breakfast Bowl
- **Lunch:** Spinach and Feta Stuffed Bell Peppers

- **Dinner:** Lemon Herb Baked Salmon with Roasted Brussels Sprouts
- **Snacks:** Apple Slices with Almond Butter

Day 30:

- **Breakfast:** Oat and Banana
- **Lunch:** Greek Salad with Grilled Chicken
- **Dinner:** Spaghetti Squash with Tomato Basil Sauce
- **Snacks:** Greek Yogurt Parfait with Mixed Berries

Day 31:

- **Breakfast:** Mango Coconut Chia Pudding
- **Lunch:** Quinoa and Black Bean Wrap with Avocado
- **Dinner:** Baked Cod with Lemon and Dill, served with Quinoa
- **Snacks:** Trail Mix with Walnuts and Dried Cranberries

Day 32:

- **Breakfast:** Sweet Potato and Kale Frittata
- **Lunch:** Chickpea and Vegetable Stir-Fry
- **Dinner:** Grilled Shrimp Skewers with Zucchini Noodles
- **Snacks:** Sliced Cucumber with Hummus

Day 33:

- **Breakfast:** Almond Flour Banana Muffins
- **Lunch:** Caprese Salad with Balsamic Glaze
- **Dinner:** Quinoa-Stuffed Bell Peppers with Turkey
- **Snacks:** Fresh Pineapple Chunks

Day 34:

- **Breakfast:** Raspberry Almond Smoothie Bowl
- **Lunch:** Lentil and Vegetable Curry
- **Dinner:** Baked Chicken Breast with Herbed Quinoa
- **Snacks:** Greek Yogurt with Honey and Pistachios

Day 35:

- **Breakfast:** Apple Cinnamon Overnight Oats
- **Lunch:** Mediterranean Chickpea Salad Wrap
- **Dinner:** Grilled Vegetable and Brown Rice Bowl
- **Snacks:** Mixed Berries with a Dollop of Greek Yogurt

Day 36:

- **Breakfast:** Quinoa Porridge with Mixed Berries
- **Lunch:** Turkey and Avocado Lettuce Wraps
- **Dinner:** Lemon Garlic Shrimp Stir-Fry with Brown Rice
- **Snacks:** Sliced Kiwi with Almonds

Day 37:

- **Breakfast:** Pumpkin Seed Granola with Yogurt
- **Lunch:** Quinoa and Chickpea Salad
- **Dinner:** Grilled Salmon with Mango Salsa and Steamed Asparagus
- **Snacks:** Fresh Melon Cubes

Additional Considerations:

- Stay hydrated with water, herbal teas, or infused water with citrus slices.
- Experiment with different fruits, vegetables, and whole grains for variety.

- Adjust portion sizes based on individual needs and activity levels.

- Feel free to swap meals or snacks based on personal preferences.

This 30-day plus meal plan offers a diverse range of flavors and nutrients while adhering to low-nickel principles. Remember to listen to your body, enjoy the culinary journey, and celebrate the positive impact of nourishing yourself with delicious and healthful meals.

CHAPTER ELEVEN
THE NICKEL FREEDOM CHART

Quick References for Informed Decision-Making

Introduction: Welcome to your essential toolkit for empowered decision-making – "Quick References for Informed Decision-Making." These concise guides are meticulously designed to be your trusted companions, offering swift insights across various life domains.

Section 1: Nutritional Wisdom at a Glance Navigate the world of nutrition effortlessly. This section provides quick references on essential nutrients, portion control, and maintaining a health-conscious diet without sacrificing taste.

Section 2: Financial Clarity in a Flash Secure your financial well-being with ease. This section offers rapid tips on budgeting, saving, and making smart financial decisions to navigate the complexities of personal finance.

Section 3: Communication Mastery Made Simple Enhance your communication skills with ease. Discover quick strategies for clear, respectful, and impactful communication in both professional and personal spheres.

Section 4: Time Management Hacks for Efficiency Optimize your productivity with time management hacks. Quick tips on prioritization, goal setting, and achieving a healthy work-life balance empower you to make the most of your time.

Section 5: Decisiveness in Stressful Moments Face stress with confidence using decisive techniques. Learn quick methods for maintaining mindfulness and making sound decisions even under high-pressure circumstances.

Section 6: Digital Well-being Unveiled Cultivate a healthy digital lifestyle effortlessly. Quick references for managing screen time, protecting your digital identity, and maintaining a balanced relationship with technology ensure a mindful and intentional approach.

Conclusion: Your journey to informed decision-making begins here, guided by these indispensable quick references. Dive into these succinct guides and embrace the efficiency of making well-informed decisions across various facets of your life.

Ready to navigate life's complexities with confidence? Let these quick references be your steadfast allies in the pursuit of intentional and informed living.

Food To Avoid and Food To Eat

While nickel can be used in the manufacturing of different items, it can also be found in many foods including some vegetables, grains, and fruits.

Although many people develop nickel allergies from consuming certain amounts of foods high in nickel, the moderate consumption of food that contains nickel can however wield some benefits for our body. It can help to improve the amount of iron that is absorbed by our body from the foods we consume and may also aid the production of red blood cells.

Nickel is widely known as one of the most common metals that causes metal allergies. A nickel allergy develops when the immune system responds adversely to encountering a product or item that contains nickel. Naturally, the immune system must protect the body from substances that can cause any harm to it such as bacteria and viruses; but, if one has a nickel allergy, the immune system can interpret nickel as a dangerous element. When your immune system sees nickel as being dangerous, it then releases certain chemicals to fight against it, and this can cause an allergic reaction.

To reduce the symptoms of a nickel allergy, your best bet is to decrease or avoid anything that can further expose you to the metal. Here are a few ways that you can reduce your nickel sensitivity.

- Instead of using clothing fasteners such as zippers and belt buckles that are made with nickel, opt for ones that are plastic coated.

- Do not choose pieces of jewelry that are made with nickel or are stainless steel plated.

- When purchasing household items like cooking utensils, razors, and keys, choose items that are not made with nickel.

- Protect your electronic devices such as laptops and phones with a protective cover.

- If you develop a rash around your hand because you made use of an object containing nickel, try to embrace a low-nickel diet.

- If you mistakenly encounter an object that is nickel-plated, wash every part of your body that it might have touched.

If you are already having allergies from using items that contain nickel, eating foods that are rich in nickel can set off your immune system and cause more symptoms. Symptoms like stomachache and skin rashes may appear and this is why you need to reduce or eliminate the consumption of foods high in nickel from your diet.

The amount of nickel that is present in foods depends on the class of the plants and the level of nickel content in the soil. For seafood, the level of nickel present can be determined by the aquatic environment. Some foods can, however, contain higher levels of nickel than others. When these foods are consumed by someone sensitive to nickel, it can aggravate their symptoms. Here are 10 foods high in nickel:

1. Vegetables

Although not all vegetables contain nickel, some vegetables, especially green ones, have been found to contain higher levels of nickel. The consumption of these vegetables should be reduced if you have a nickel allergy. These vegetables include lettuce, cabbage, spinach, kale, leeks, and bean sprouts.

2. Nuts and seeds

Certain nuts and seeds are known to contain significant amounts of nickel, so it is recommended that you eat them in moderation. Such nuts and seeds include sesame seeds, pistachio, walnuts, sunflower seeds, melon seeds, hazelnuts, almonds, melon seeds.

3. Whole grains and wheat

Products of whole grains like whole-grain bread is an example of foods high in nickel. Research has shown that a kilogram of wheat flour contains about 1270 milligrams of nickel. Cereals are also included in this category, although not all cereals are rich in nickel. Other whole grains and wheat that contain nickel include chocolate cereals, barley, millet, pearl, chocolate oat bars, unpolished rice, wheat germ, buckwheat, and rye products.

4. Canned foods

When a substance is stored for a long time inside a can, the chances that it will contain nickel and other sensitive metal substances is very high. Canned foods that should be avoided include canned nuts, pickles, fizzy drinks, tomato paste, fish and meat, and other canned foods.

5. Legumes

Lentils, peanuts, chickpeas, soybeans, and other soy products like tofu and soy milk are some of the legumes that have high levels of nickel in them. The consumption of these foods can trigger your symptoms if you already have a nickel allergy.

6. Certain fruits

Fruits are generally healthy and as such, you can consume them safely. However, some fruits are rich in nickel and can actuate a nickel allergy. Such fruits include prunes, pineapple, oranges, figs, avocados, bananas, pears, dates, raspberries, and canned fruits.

7. Cocoa products and chocolates

Cocoa products and chocolates have high levels of nickel. Chocolates are made from cocoa beans and cocoa beans possess fat; this fat can increase the reaction of your immune system. Some pastries and milk also contain nickel. With a nickel allergy, you should avoid hot cocoa, every type of licorice, chocolate-flavored drinks, chocolate milk, and other products that contain cocoa.

8. Cashews

Although cashews have a lot of benefits for the body as they can prevent gallstones and help to maintain healthy bones and muscles, they are relatively high in nickel.

9. Seafood

Some types of fish contain high amounts of nickel; they can have up to 0.08 milligrams. Shellfish and fresh-water fish should be avoided. Other fish to eliminate from your diet include scarps, breams, crawfish, white suckers, mussels, roaches, bass, and shrimps.

10. Condiments and spices

Some spices and condiments also have high levels of nickel and their consumption should be reduced if you are looking to alleviate the symptoms of a nickel allergy. Condiments and spices in this category include juniper, cumin, cinnamon, Popeye seeds, and carnations.

Other foods that are high in nickel

Other foods that are high in nickel include instant coffee powders, teas, and some types of margarine. Rather than consuming the above foods that contain high levels of nickel that can trigger your allergy, you should opt for these foods below instead:

Foods That Are Low In Nickel And Good For Consumption

1. Certain fruits

Strawberries, apples, grapes, peaches, blueberries, raisins, and blackberries are all examples of fruits that do not contain nickel. Make sure you don't consume canned ones. You can eat these fruits cooked or fresh.

2. Plain dairy products

Yogurt, butter, cheese, and plain milk possess low levels of nickel. You can consume these plain dairy products even with an allergy.

3. Refined grains

Although buckwheat, oat bran, oatmeal, and wheat bran are great foods that you can get fiber from, they are high in nickel. Instead of consuming them, you should instead eat refined grains in your diet such as refined corn products like corn flakes, polished rice, and refined white flour.

4. Lean meat

You should incorporate lean cuts of pork, meat, and chicken into your diet as they are low in nickel. However, when preparing these lean cuts of meat, avoid cooking them with utensils that are made with nickel.

5. Root vegetables

For people who are sensitive to nickel, it is advised that you go for root vegetables rather than green vegetables. Root vegetables that are low in nickel include carrots, sweet potatoes, onions, potatoes, and beets.

Although the best way by which you can prevent the advent of a nickel allergy is to avoid items that contain it, you can't completely halt your consumption of some foods that contain nickel. The key to solving this problem is to consume foods high in nickel in moderation. Endeavor to limit your intake of foods high in nickel. Notwithstanding, eliminate the usage of nickel-plated products; make sure you check the label of items before purchasing them to know if they were produced using nickel. Instead of using items that contain nickel, opt for items that are made with brass, silicone, and titanium.

CONCLUSION:

In the culmination of Becky Mathew-Smith's culinary odyssey, "The Low-Nickel Diet Cookbook for Beginners" stands as a beacon of holistic well-being and resilient living. Through the inspiring journey of Emily, a 32-year-old who conquered the challenges of nickel allergy, and the expert guidance of Becky, this book transcends the realm of traditional cookbooks.

The narrative begins with the Nickel Odyssey, chronicling the intricacies of managing nickel allergies. Emily's triumph over adversity becomes a symbol of resilience and hope, setting the stage for a culinary transformation led by Becky. Each recipe within the cookbook is a testament to mindful ingredients, flavor-packed dishes, and a celebration of health-conscious cooking that doesn't compromise on taste.

Beyond the kitchen, the book dives into holistic insights, offering readers a comprehensive understanding of low nickel living. From the impact of various foods on nickel absorption to practical tips for dining out and socializing, Becky Mathew-Smith provides a wealth of knowledge to empower readers in their health journey.

The cookbook not only serves as a practical guide with over 100 tantalizing recipes tailored for low-nickel diets but also offers a 30-day meal plan for seamless integration into daily life. The Low-Nickel Diet Chart becomes an invaluable resource, aiding readers in making informed choices whether cooking at home or dining out.

"Low Nickel Diet Cookbook for Beginners" is more than just a collection of recipes; it's a source of inspiration, a beacon of hope, and a comprehensive guide for reclaiming health. As readers turn the pages, they embark on a transformative journey, guided by the expertise of Becky Mathew-Smith and the uplifting story of Emily. This cookbook invites individuals to not only embrace a low-nickel diet but to thrive, celebrating a life of vibrant health and well-being.

Printed in Great Britain
by Amazon